Secrets About Writing And Publishing Your Book:
What Other Publishers Will Not Tell You

By
Dr. Mary J. Ogenaarekhua

Dedication

As in my other books, I dedicate this book to God the Father, God the Son and God the Holy Ghost. Lord God, You gave me the words to write in this book. As it is written in Psalm 68:11, so You have done concerning this book:

> *"The Lord gave the word: great was the company of those that published it."*

Thanks Father, for making me a scribe in Your kingdom and for giving me the grace to write what You gave me. I know that it is by Your grace that I write and I give You all the glory for all the words in this book.

May they help many people to learn how to write and how to get their manuscripts published. You are the best Father and Teacher and I love You.

As always, I thank You for giving me To His Glory Publishing Company and for making it a great publishing company. Father, to You be all the glory in Jesus name.

Secrets About Writing And Publishing Your Book:
What Other Publishers Will Not Tell You

Published by: To His Glory Publishing Company, Inc.
463 Dogwood Drive, NW
Lilburn, GA 30047
(770) 458-7947
www.tohisglorypublishing.com
www.maryjministries.org

Copyright 2009© Mary J. Ogenaarekhua. All rights reserved. No part of this book may be reproduced or retransmitted in any form or by any means without the written permission of the author or the publisher.

This book is available at:
Amazon.com, BarnesandNoble.com, Borders.com,
Booksamillion.com, etc.,
and in the UK and Canada.

Also, you can order this book with the
Order Form at the back of this book or contact:
www.tohisglorypublishing.com
(770) 458-7947

ISBN: 978-0-9821900-2-9 or 0-9821900-2-6

Table of Contents

Preface 11
Acknowledgements 13
A Note from the Author 15

Chapter 1
A Word about the Publishing Industry 17
Traditional Publishing 17
Print-On-Demand (POD) 17
Publishers Want Books that Will Sell 18
Criteria for Submitting Your Book 19
Manuscript Format for POD Books 20
International Standard Book Number (ISBN) 20
Library of Congress Number 21

Chapter 2
Working with Major Distributors 23
Dealing With Rejection of Manuscripts 24
Importance of Name Recognition 25
Obtaining Funds to Publish Your Book 27
Book Distribution 29
Self-Publishing 29

Chapter 3
Copyrights and Copyright Issues 31
Obtaining Copyrights 31
Things that Make Obtaining Permission Tedious 36
Showing How You Use Quoted Materials 37
The Blessing of Paraphrasing 39
Storing Your Permission Granted Letter 39
Questions and Answers about Copyrights 41
Books in the Public Domain 42
Obtaining Book Reviews 47
Purposes of Book Reviews 48
Obtaining a Foreword for Your Book 49

Warning about Responses to Your Request 51
Only Send Out Edited Materials for Reviews 53
A Word about Your Reviews 53

Chapter 4
Positioning Your Book for Marketing 55
Questions and Answers about Marketing 58

Chapter 5
Basic Rules About Choosing Your Topic 63
Collecting Your Thoughts 63
Research Your Chosen Topic 63
Have a Unique Perspective on Your Chosen Topic 64
Getting the Attention of the Potential Book Buyer 65
Writing About Secular Subjects 66
Selecting Your Title 67
The Importance of Colors 68
Questions and Answers about Color and Artwork 70

Chapter 6
Your Book Size, Layout, and Formatting 75
Book Size 75
Pocket Size Books 75
About Large Size Books 76
My Observation at a Book Sale Table 77
Book Layout 77
Creating a Fair Size Book 79
Book Formatting 79
Paperback vs. Hardback Books 80
Using Images inside Your Book 81
Using the Proper Tab Key 81
Using the Bold Key 82

Chapter 7
The Art of Writing 85
Ghost Writing 85

Writing as an Art 85
Writing with a Purpose 86
Have a Book Outline 87

Chapter 8
Understanding the Parts of Your Book 89
The Book Spine 89
The Title Page 89
The Endorsement Page 90
The Publisher Page 90
The Dedication Page 91
The Acknowledgement Page 91
The Foreword Page 91
The Introduction or Preface page 92
The Table of Contents Page(s) 92
The Chapters in Your Book 93
The Conclusion Page(s) 93
The Bibliography Page(s) 94
The Advertisement Page(s) 94
Bookstore Order Form 95

Chapter 9
Summary of the Basic Rules of Grammar 97
Parts of Speech 97
Nouns 99
Objects 101
Pronouns 103
Verbs 105
Verb Tenses 108
Adverbs 109
Adjectives 110
Prepositions 111
Conjunctions 112
Interjections 113
Clauses 113

Chapter 10
Use of Punctuation Marks 117
Why Use Punctuation Marks? 117
Use of Commas, Dashes, Hyphen, Colons,
Semicolons and Periods 118

Chapter 11
Basic Rules about Editing Your Book.................. 121
Types of Editing 121
The Importance of a Well Written Manuscript 122
How to Save Money on Extensive Editing 124
What to Edit For 125
Words of Wisdom about Editing 125

Conclusion 129
Bibliography 131

Preface

To me, writing is one of the most exciting and enduring things that you will ever do but it requires work. Nothing happens until you actually put your thoughts down on paper but the good news is that published books can still be around hundreds of years after you are gone! People can still find out about your thoughts and ideology as they read the topics that you wrote about years after you have passed on. This in itself should be a motivating factor for people to put their thoughts down on paper.

Because English Grammar and English Composition are not most people's favorite subjects in high school and college, a lot of people do not think that they can actually write something that other people might be interested in reading. If you are one of such people, I have good news for you. Writing is an art and you are never too late to learn it. All it requires from you is a willingness to learn and the discipline to actually sit down and write. What you think is trivia might be someone's life changing instruction, direction or words of wisdom.

This book is meant to be a learning tool and it is designed to help those who are thinking about writing, in the process of writing, or have written a manuscript that they would like to see published. It will walk the reader through the entire process of writing, editing and getting his or her manuscript published. It is my desire that after you have read this book, you will become well informed about how to write an effective manuscript and about the publishing industry.

Remember, nothing happens until you actually write your thoughts down on a piece of paper. Unless you have money to pay a "ghost writer" to write your book for you, the information in this book will help you become a good writer.

Acknowledgements

Thank You Lord for giving me the grace to write this book; to You be all the glory.

Thank you **Lynne Garbinsky** for helping me to transcribe, organize and edit these materials. May God richly bless you.

I also thank **Dee Little** for her work in editing this book. I truly appreciate you.

I thank all the participants in my writing seminars and conferences. Many of you requested to have the materials that are presented in this book published so that you can get your hands on a copy. Therefore, I appreciate all your persistence in placing a demand on me to write this book. I hope it helps you tremendously.

A Note from the Author

I believe that the materials in this book will benefit anyone who is planning to write or who is in the process of writing a book. I was an author years before I became a publisher and as a new author, there were things that I had to find out the hard way.

Therefore, I am hoping that this book will help many to avoid some of the things that made the publishing of my first book a long and tedious process. As you read this book, I want you to always bear in mind that I was an author before I became a publisher. As a result, I am speaking to the reader from my experience as an author as well as a publisher.

Note: *The materials in this book were first presented in classrooms, seminars and conference settings. As a result, some of the chapters have a question and answer session at the end. These are actual questions asked by students and conference attendees.*

Chapter 1

A Word about the Publishing Industry

The publishing industry is vast and each publisher will offer you a variety of services. The good news about publishing today is that you can now choose between the traditional way of publishing and the new way of publishing. They are both discussed below.

Traditional Publishing

There is what we call traditional publishing and it refers to those companies that will publish your book and house copies of your book in a warehouse or print a limited edition of your book each time you place an order. This type of publishing is very expensive because it costs a lot of money to store your books in a warehouse and if you have to print a limited edition, you may have to buy several thousand copies of your book at one time.

As a result, many authors needed to have an average of $15,000 just to have one book published. Even if you had the money, your book still stands a good chance of being rejected because of scarcity of warehouse space. With this type of system, only proven authors (people who have written books that are considered best sellers) are paid the most attention by publishers. This is changing because of the new method of publishing that is now available.

Print-On-Demand (POD)

This new method of publishing is called Print-On-Demand (POD) and it is making the cost of publishing a book affordable to most people. The reason is because you are not required to store your book in a publisher's warehouse nor are you required to buy thousands of copies of your book at one time!

Rather, the publisher allows you to buy fewer copies of your book and your book is stored digitally in an electronic version so that it is ever ready to be printed when someone places an order for it. This way, your book is never out of print because it can be stored for years in an electronic version for the major online bookstores like Amazon.com. When someone orders a book, it is printed and shipped to the person within a few days!

Publishers Want Books that Will Sell

Publishers are in business to make money and as a result, no publisher wants a book that will only appeal to the author and the author's immediate family. Publishing is big business and big business cares about putting a product on the market that can give them control of the book market or bring in a fair share of the book market. Therefore, almost all publishers are looking for a potential best seller! There is a high rejection rate in the publishing industry. About 80-90% of the manuscripts submitted to traditional publishers are rejected each year. The reason is because no publisher wants to invest time in a book that has no potential for good sales. No one wants a book that will go no where.

Also as an author, you do not want to spend your time and money to produce a book that no one outside of your immediate family thinks is worth reading. You want your book to be well received by just about anyone who picks it up. As a result, I always advise writers to choose a topic that would cause the general public to become interested in their work even if they are writing their biographies.

I am the CEO of **To His Glory Publishing Company**

and we have gone through many manuscripts that made us wonder what the goal of the writers were and we came away disappointed because the manuscripts were really "nothing about nothing." We just wondered what motivated the people to want to write because there was no clear motive for writing, no clear topic and no identifiable purpose for writing the books. Therefore, I say to you, do not let your writing be "nothing about nothing." Make sure that the topic you choose to write on has a targeted audience and make sure that you are writing with a purpose in mind.

Criteria for Submitting Your Book

There are some publishing houses that do not want you to submit a fully written manuscript to them. They prefer that you send them an outline so that they can guide you through the writing process while others will accept a fully written manuscript. You need to find out what the publishing house that you have selected requires.

Most publishing houses require that your book be submitted in a Microsoft Word document. You will be surprised to learn about the number of people that want to submit their manuscripts in several different forms, but the industry standard is a Microsoft Word document with a 12 point font and in Book Antigua.

There are other fonts out there for authors to choose from but be aware that not all fonts are free. If you choose a font that is not free to be used in publishing, you might find yourself having to pay for the right to use the font. Not too long ago, I decided to create a daily journal to go with my Visions and Dreams Manual and text book (**Keys to Understanding Your Visions and Dreams and A Teacher's Manual on Visions and Dreams**) and I chose a very fancy font that curls and that was really pretty. When I found out how much it would cost me to purchase and have the font downloaded to me, I immediately chose a font that I knew was free of charge!

Also, when it comes to manufacturing the book, the printers might not be willing to purchase the font just for your book. We have had books rejected and sent back by the printers who place the books on Amazon.com and Barnesandnoble.com because the fonts chosen by the authors were not available for free. Therefore, you need to be careful when it comes to choosing the fonts for the inside of your book. Again, some fancy fonts cost money and they add to the total cost of publishing your book.

The fonts for the **book covers** are usually free of charge. The printers can easily work with those because the entire cover can be treated like a graphic image but the book interior (inside) is a different matter. The best thing to do is to make sure that you write your book in Book Antigua in order to avoid complication down the road.

Manuscript Format for POD Books

For Print-on-Demand books (POD), please keep the format of your book simple. Some people put text boxes, jazzy characters and images in their manuscripts and they think that they have correctly formatted their documents. They forget one thing; that is, most publishers work with major distributors who actually manufacture the books to industry standards. Therefore, publishing houses have to format your book according to the required specifications for your book size.

International Standard Book Number (ISBN)

The United States government requires every book to have an International Standard Book Number. It is called an **ISBN**, for short. There is a company that sells these numbers for the government. Usually, the publisher will assign an ISBN to your book but you can also buy a bulk of ISBN numbers if you are going to write several books. They are not sold individually and each book can only have one ISBN. This number is used to identify your book in every place where books are cataloged. Bookstores look up books in their computer systems using the ISBN, the book title or the author's name.

Library of Congress Number

Just like the ISBN, the Library of Congress Number is also used to catalog your book in the United States Library of Congress book catalog system as well as other libraries. This is a useful number for those who are writing academic books that have to be cataloged in college libraries or public libraries. It is not a mandated number by the US government for every book published in the United States. Therefore, you do not have to get it if you do not need it.

I was not aware of this when I published my very first book years ago. I paid for a Library of Congress Number and I did not find out that I did not need it until years later. You do not need to get the Library of Congress Number if your book is not an academic book that needs to be included in the catalog of books in libraries.

Chapter 2

Working with Major Distributors

We happen to work with one of the biggest printing and distribution companies in the United States, Canada and the United Kingdom. What the big distributors do is work with publishing houses such as **To His Glory Publishing Company** to print and distribute books. It is the publishing houses that edit, format, layout, design cover, etc., to make the manuscript ready for production. Because we use the POD system of publishing, we then forward the manuscript to the major distributor for book production and catalog.

Although these major distributors work with the publishing houses, they do not involve themselves in the preparation stages of the manuscript. Their job is to print the book, make sure it is on the online bookstores and that it is positioned for major distribution if the need arises. Book distribution is a different service from publishing. I will address that later.

As you can see from the above, it is the publishing houses that actually sit down with the authors in order to create the book and to do everything that is necessary to get the book ready for printing and distribution. Once the major distributors receive the manuscript, they will actually manufacture the book. They will see to it that the book is displayed on Amazon.com, Barnesandnoble.com and they will also see to it that when someone orders your book on Amazon.com or any of the online bookstores or retail outlets that your book is actually printed and sent to the buyer without any problem.

If your book becomes a best seller or your book is selling well, the major distributors are well positioned to get the book out there to where it is needed. For instance, it only takes a buyer a few days to order a book through Amazon.com or through Barnesandnoble.com and the books are guaranteed not to go out of print! This is why self-published books cannot be marketed because they have no distribution set up or avenue to be mass marketed.

Dealing With Rejection of Manuscripts

As I stated before, with traditional publishing houses, about eighty to ninety percent (80-90%) of the manuscripts that are submitted to them are rejected. The rejection rate is so high because as I told you in Chapter 1, publishing houses are in business to make money and they want known authors whose books will sell. From their perspective, if nobody knows you, who then is going to buy your book? Would you invest your money in someone whose book will only sell fifty copies? This is one of the major reasons why eighty to ninety percent of manuscripts are rejected by publishers.

You do not have to take it personally if your manuscript is rejected by a publisher. You have to act on some of the input or feedback that you get from them. If you did not receive any feedback, then keep trying till you find a publisher that is willing to work with you. **To His Glory Publishing Company** has helped so many authors who were rejected by other publishers. This, of course, required a lot of time in reorganizing, rewriting and editing on our part to make the manuscript presentable. We help writers make their work presentable in order to bring God glory.

This is one of the reasons that we are in business. Therefore, do not become discouraged if your manuscript is not accepted by the initial publishers that you contacted. Instead, remember that they are in business to make money and they are looking for people who have already built followers for themselves and who can help them bring in a lot of revenue.

For instance, if a well known movie star, an Ex-President of the United States or another famous person asks me to publish his or her book; I can prepare to be living in Hawaii at the end of the year. Why? Because, publishing such a book is like hitting a jackpot. Books by such people will sell at least a million copies. This is why publishing houses are willing to give such people money in advance for them to produce a manuscript. They know that when the book sells and they subtract the amount that they paid the writer upfront, they can still make millions of dollars. The book will continue to generate revenue from which they can continue to pay the author more royalties.

This is why you see that United States Presidents are given millions of dollars by publishing houses when they leave office to write their memoirs. Such books usually sell millions of copies because the general public is anxiously awaiting such memoirs to be published. They become best sellers in the very first weeks of their release. The money paid to the Ex-Presidents is usually recouped within a few weeks because people are looking forward to such books. People usually come out en masse to buy these types of books but if you are talking about an average Joe on the street that nobody knows, you will have a hard sale with his book because nobody knows him.

Actually, most traditional publishing houses want you to submit to them a survey that shows how much percentage of the book reading market you already control. In other words, they want people whose names the general public already knows. This is why I tell authors to work on building "name recognition" for themselves.

Importance of Name Recognition

Name recognition is very important in the book, recording and movie industries. Once the public recognizes you in any of these businesses, they will be more willing to invest their money in what you have to offer them. This is why you have to work on making your name known out there in the market. For a first time writer, it means a willingness to aggressively promote your first book in any media outlet that is available to you.

Once you have created a "market share" for yourself, you are at liberty just like some very famous authors, to decide various things concerning your books. Until then, you have to use wisdom by recognizing ways that you can pursue the promotion and marketing of your book. You also cannot allow your book to become too big. For instance, a famous author such as Stephen King can release big books because he has a huge market. He is able to do this because those who read his books know who Stephen King is and they want what he is dishing out to them in his books. The size of the books no longer matter to the reader because they enjoy the books and are willing to sacrifice the time to finish the books.

If an unknown author tries to do what Stephen King does, they will not get the same result. I mean, you just put the same type of book next to Stephen King's and see if your book sells as fast as his does. Therefore, you first want to introduce yourself to the reading public by working on building name recognition. It is like wooing people; you want to create a name for yourself first with your initial books.

Once you have built a name, then people will begin to expect your written materials. Most famous authors get paid to write but it was not always like that for many of them. Most new writers do not know this so they come to our publishing company expecting to be paid for their manuscript that has not yet been tested. This is one of the pitfalls in publishing because many people believe that just because they put some ideas down on a piece of paper, they are immediately going to get lots of money.

A lady once looked at me and said during our conversation, "You mean, I have to pay you to publish my book?" I said, "Yes, because if we were to go out there and stand in front of Wal-Mart and mention your name, people would not know who you are. Your writing may not appeal to people beyond your immediate family members." As it turned out, she only had twelve pages of manuscript that she wanted us to pay her for! You have to educate yourself about the publishing industry.

Obtaining Funds to Publish Your Book

Another category that we want to look at when it comes to publishing your book is obtaining funds. This is where a lot of people get stuck concerning their manuscript because they do not go further in their attempt to become published authors. When you study economics, you will discover that there is a thing called "effective demand." A demand is not considered a serious demand until it becomes effective. An effective demand is a demand that is backed by the ability to pay.

In other words, to show that you really want to buy or do something, you have to put your money where your mouth is. This also applies to those who want to publish their manuscripts because you can have a very good idea and you can even finish a manuscript but if you do not have funds for publishing, it could be on your shelf for a long time. This means that it will not go anywhere.

One of the ways that some of our authors overcame the hurdle of funds for publishing was to inform members of their families, friends and colleagues that they needed funds for publishing their manuscript. Someone actually gave one of our authors $10,000 towards publishing his book! Of course, we did not even charge him half that amount but he made money for himself by letting people know that he needed funds for his book.

He sent letters to his friends, to people that he knew, to members of his family and to the core group that he ministers to. He told them that he was in the process of completing his book and that he needed funds. He gave them an outline of what the book was about. You have to come up with ways that you can generate money to publish your book and not let lack of finances defeat you. You may not have the money but someone who does might be willing to give it to you if they see that your book is for a good cause.

Another Apostle sent a letter to the people in his network asking for a donation towards getting his book published. His letter stated that he needed $15,000 to get his book published. Someone who knew about our publishing company sent him an email telling him to go to: **To His Glory Publishing Company** and get his book published for much less. He was amazed to find out that it would cost him less than $4,000 to get his book published by us!

One way to obtain funds is to save up the money. Some people have very good jobs or well established businesses that make publishing fees seem like nothing to them. You are blessed if you happen to be one of such people but if you are not; then you have to try and raise the money. As I stated above, one of the ways to do this is by a letter of intent. You can send it to all the people that are within your sphere of influence as well as your family members.

You can also send it to your email group informing them about your manuscript and that you need their help in raising the funds to publish it. You may be pleasantly surprised at the responses that you might receive, but if you do not take the first step, no one would know about your need. Therefore, it is up to you to take the initial step because you never know who God might move upon to help you out.

You can even ask your pastor or somebody to help you put together a fund raising event in order to raise money towards getting your book published. As I said earlier, if people find out that you are writing something that is really significant and that is going to be life impacting, they may support you.

Also, find out if there are organizations that are giving out grants for the topic that you choose. There may be organizations out there that may be willing to support you if the topic you are writing on is something that they sponsor. Therefore, do some research to see what types of grants, if any, are available for the topic you have chosen.

Book Distribution

There are companies in the United States that buy books. **These companies buy books for their chains of Christian bookstores, major bookstores and other book distribution outlets across the nation.** They will actually review each book to see if it is suitable for their outlet stores. When a book is selected, they will purchase copies of the book for all their outlet stores across the nation.

These companies have relationships with major book distribution companies that they already have "purchase contracts" with and they do not work with self-published books. In other words, they do not deal with books that are self-published. As a new author, you must therefore make sure that your book is well positioned for distribution. You also must make sure that you can sell your book through the major online bookstores like Amazon.com and Barnesandnoble.com, Booksamillion.com, etc.

Self-Publishing

Many people write a book and they have a printing company print copies of the book for them. This is called self-publishing. They do not go through a proper book publishing company and as a result, the book is not set up for proper distribution. The reason that most distributors do not work with self-published books is because books that are self-published lack continuity of life and because they have not been set up for major distribution. In other words, self-published books can easily go out of print, they are not cataloged anywhere so that a book buyer can be guaranteed to have easy access to them. There is no guarantee of supply when needed.

Most people who self-publish their books end up with hundreds or thousands of copies of their books in their garages with no avenue to mass market them. I do not recommend self-publishing because of the simple reason that you will not be able to market self-published books. I have had people who self-published their books contact me because they want me to help market their books but there is no way to market self-published books.

The truth of the matter is that major book buyers prefer to work with major book distributors and not with individual authors. Therefore, there is no room for self-published books in the way the publishing industry is set up. Again, major companies prefer to deal with other major companies and not individual authors.

Chapter 3

Copyrights and Copyright Issues

Obtaining Copyrights

Copyrights are some of the major issues in publishing. You cannot just quote someone's material and think that it is OK. Just like songs, books are covered by the US copyrights laws. In order to quote from someone's book, you have to ask the person for permission. I discovered during the process of writing my first book that getting copyright permission can be a very tedious process. The book would have been twice its current size but I encountered some copyright permission issues that made me to remove some of the material that I wanted to use in the book.

One of the authors whose material I had really enjoyed and quoted extensively refused to give me permission to quote from his work. I had written almost thirty pages in support of his argument using different quotes from his book to advance my point of view. I had to delete those pages from the book.

Another author who finally got back to me did it on his death bed. According to his daughter, signing the Permission Granted Form was one of the last things he did before he expired. His daughter took my request to the hospital and said, "Daddy there is some author in Atlanta who wants to quote from your book." She said it made her dad very happy and he got up and signed the Permission Form. She called me to let me know that my request really encouraged her dad on his death bed. I was surprised and thankful because if I had not acted when I did, he would not have been able to sign the form before he died.

I had also used a picture of the Madonna from a major publisher's encyclopedia and when I contacted them for permission to use the images; it took them almost nine months to get back to me. When they did, they wanted me to tell them how much my book would be priced and how many copies of it would be printed so that they could determine what to charge me for the first prints. According to them, if I decide to print more copies at a later date, I would have to resubmit a new permission request. This meant that I would have had to pay them every single time I wanted to print more copies of my book.

My book was already published four months before I heard from them. When I realized that they were holding up the release of my book, I found a young man who knew how to draw and he drew a picture of the Madonna for me. He did not even do it for the money but I gave him fifty dollars and it solved my problem.

I also discovered that one of the major greeting card sellers in the United States does not give anyone outside of its company permission to use any of the images on the greeting cards. I had also requested permission from them and it was denied. As a result, I always advise new authors to get an artist to draw an image for them in order to avoid the rigmarole over copyright. There are also online companies that sell graphic images. I find them to be the best source for images or artworks. You can buy from them artwork that they own the copyright to and not have to worry about copyright issues.

We had an author who wanted to use some really fancy original artwork or painting. She did not want to buy an image online so we sent her to a professional artist. The artist gave her a price quote of about $3,000 for a single painting. She then decided that is was OK to buy an image online.

As you can see, there are easy solutions to overcoming the copyright hurdles for graphics or images but when it comes to quoting from other people's work, even before you finish the manuscript, you need to immediately send the person whose work you are quoting from an email. I discovered that if you write them a letter and they have no idea who you are, they do not get back to you for a long time and some for one year or more. As a result, I now send out emails to request permissions. I drafted two letters that I usually send out when requesting permission. One is **Permission Request** to use quoted materials from their book and the next letter is a draft of their **Permission Granted Letter** that I want them to sign and mail back to me. If I have to mail the request form, I usually enclose a stamped, self-addressed envelope so that all the person has to do is just sign under the wording **I grant you permission to quote from my book** _____ and then mail it back to me.

Dr. Mary J. Ogenaarekhua

Sample: Permission Request Form

Permission Request Form

Mary J. Ogenaarekhua
463 Dogwood Drive, NW
Lilburn, GA 30047

Date:

To:

_____
_____
_____

Re: Request for written permission to use attached quotations from your book, _____.

Dear Sir/Madam:

I am requesting written permission to use quotations from your book, _____ in my upcoming book titled: **Unveiling the God-Mother** and to retain the quotations in any future revisions or editions of the book.

I have enclosed a self-address stamped envelope and a Permission Granted Form in this letter for your convenience. You only have to sign and return it me.

Thank you very much for your immediate attention to this matter.

Sincerely,

Mary J. Ogenaarekhua

Never forget to attach the quotation, image or graphic that you are requesting permission for.

Sample: Permission Granted Form

Permission Granted Form

Date:

To: Mary Ogenaarekhua
     463 Dogwood Dr., NW
     Lilburn, GA 30047

From:
_____
_____
_____

Dear Ms. Ogenaarekhua:

I hereby grant you copy-right/permission to use quotation/my name/ picture in the USA edition of your book titled: _____. You may also use this permission in all subsequent revisions and editions of the book.

Sincerely,

_____   Signature Here

_____   Print Name and
Title Here

The reason that I do this is because I also discovered that some people may not want to be bothered because of their busy schedules and because there is no incentive for them to sit down and draft a letter to you. Therefore, getting back to you may not be a priority to them but to you, it is a priority. You do not want someone to sit on your request for nine months and thereby hold up the publication of your book.

It is the reason why I came up with the **Permission Request Form** and the **Permission Granted Form**. I saw how efficient these forms were because when I sent them to the publishers of Dake's Bible, I received the Permission Granted Form back within a week! All they had to do was sign the Permission Granted Form and send it back to me in the stamped, self-addressed envelope I had enclosed.

The major publishing houses have **Permission Departments** that handle the permission requests that come to them from around the world. Because they are answered in the order in which they are received, it can take a while for them to process your request.

Things that Make Obtaining Permission Tedious

One of the things that make obtaining permission very tedious is difficulty in tracking the rightful owner of the copyright. Some copyrights are owned by companies and because companies are bought and sold all the time, it can be very difficult to trace the rightful owner of a particular copyright. It is the rightful owner of the copyright that can grant you permission.

I remember using quotation from a book that was published by a major publishing house but when I tried to contact them for permission, I discovered that the publishing house had been bought by another publishing house. I had to go through three different companies in order to find out who was now the copyright owner of the book and this took several months.

I had another experience with Penguin Books. I quoted from a book that was published by Penguin books and I discovered while I was trying to obtain permission that there was Penguin Books USA, Penguin Books Canada, Penguin Books UK, Penguin Books Australia, etc. It was a great task to find out which Penguin Books owned the copyright to the book that I quoted from. I had to contact them all and this took several months. Each one of them had a separate permission department because each was autonomous in granting permission. The permission departments of most publishing companies do not produce much of a profit and as a result, I believe that they are not highly staffed nor motivated to answer requests very quickly. I think that it is not a priority to them to get back to you immediately.

In my particular situation, it took Penguin Books UK a while to get back to me and they told me that they calculated the number of words that I quoted from the book. According to them, the words were less than a hundred words and as a result, I could use them without any financial charge. You can see that even when a publishing house wants to give you permission, they have to count the number of words that you used in your quotation so that they can determine how much to charge you.

Some publishing houses might allow you to quote a hundred words free-of-charge while some might want to charge you for words above fifty. Therefore, I say that it matters how many words you quote from a book when you are dealing with the bigger publishing houses.

Showing How You Use Quoted Materials

When asking an author or a publisher for permission to use quotations from their works, it is advisable to show them how you are using the quotes in your book because many people might be wondering if you are going to use their own works against them. People want to know that you are not writing to criticize what they have said or that you are not writing something derogatory about their work.

Therefore, not knowing how you are going to use the quoted materials might make them reluctant to give you permission to use them. As for me, I usually attach the quoted materials that I am asking permission to use; I actually show them an excerpt of how it appears in my book. In other words, I have one or two paragraphs that show how I am using the quotation that I am asking permission for in my book. Doing this allows them to feel comfortable about giving me permission. I encourage other writers to do the same.

However, when you are writing as a critic or writing something that is not flattering about another person's work, it is difficult for you to tell the person what you are planning to do with the quotation and this might make it difficult for the person to give you his or her permission. In fact, in this type of situation, showing how you use the quotation might actually work against you. Therefore, you have to use wisdom without lying or bending the truth about what you are doing. In this case, I go ahead and ask for permission without showing the person how I used the quote and just hope to get a favorable response.

I ran into this type of situation when I was writing my first book titled **"Unveiling the God-Mother"** and I wanted permission to use a picture of the Pope carrying the "Monstrance" (a pagan symbol). I was writing against the use of the Monstrance in the Roman Catholic Church and my point was that the Pope should not carry a pagan symbol because the Monstrance is from the Egyptian temple of the *sun god*. Therefore, when the Roman Catholic organization that owned the copyright to the image wanted me to send them an excerpt of my writing concerning the Monstrance; I did not send it to them because I did not want to lie to them. Also, I did not want them to know how I was going to use the image of the Pope carrying the Monstrance. It would have been self defeating for me to do so.

It was a very good picture of the Pope carrying the pagan symbol (the Monstrance) and I knew that they would not like what I was writing about it. It was clear that I was not writing in favor of the Monstrance and I know that some other people had also written against its use in the Roman Catholic Church. I was not surprised when they did not give me permission. What I did instead, was to have someone draw for me a picture of a priest carrying the Monstrance. I was able to use the drawing to make my point that Christians need to stay away from pagan symbols and from paganism.

The Blessing of Paraphrasing

The easiest or quickest way to get around the problem of copyright is learning how to paraphrase. Rather than quote an author's work verbatim, it is easier to paraphrase. When you paraphrase, you do not have to deal with the issues of copyright but if you use a quote from a person's book, then you need to obtain permission to use the quote or else you would be in violation of the US copyright laws.

Therefore, I say to the beginning writer, learn to paraphrase because it will save you a lot of time and money. It will eliminate any problem that might occur because of copyright laws. Before I wrote my first book, I went to the library to find out about copyright laws and the reference materials also stressed the use of paraphrasing rather a verbatim quote.

Storing Your Permission Granted Letter

Once you get all the copyright Permission Granted Forms back, please store them in a safety deposit for future reference. You need to do this because if in the future there is ever a dispute over your use of quotations from a book, you have the Permission Granted Form to legally protect you from a law suit. Many years from now, you might be gone and whoever gave you permission might also be gone and if your descendants ever get questioned by the descendants of the author whose book you quoted from, your descendants can always produce the Permission Granted Form.

I have all my copyrights and Permission Granted Forms in a safety deposit box. For example, if you look at the cover of one of my books titled, **"Keys to Successful Mentoring Relationships,"** you will see me and eight other ladies in the picture. I decided to use them on the book cover because some of them were my students in the mentoring class.

Also, when you look on the inside of the accompanying workbook titled, **"A Workbook for Successful Mentoring,"** you will see pictures of some of the students towards the end of the book. Each student that submitted a picture had an opportunity to write something about the course and what the students wrote was included in the workbook along with the picture. It was also my way of validating and positioning them for the future for whenever they decide to teach the course on mentoring.

Wherever they go to teach the course, the people will be required to use the workbook and the picture will immediately show that they received a formal training on mentoring. It will show that they did not just wake up one morning and decide that they were going to teach mentoring; rather, it will show that they know something about the subject of mentoring. It was my way of promoting them.

I attend the same church with five of these ladies but I did not say to myself that because they are my Christian sisters, it was OK to use their pictures or their reviews about the mentoring class without their permissions. Every one of them had to sign a release that said that it was OK to use her picture on the book cover and on the inside, and that it was OK to include her class review in the workbook.

The permission releases also cover all future editions or revisions of both the textbook and the workbook. You see from this example that not only did I obtain permission for the current edition of the books, but I also made sure that the permissions covered all future editions as well.

Note: *The materials in this book were first presented in a classroom setting.*

Questions and Answers about Copyrights

Below are some of the questions from the students and my accompanying answers concerning copyright issues. I hope that they will be beneficial to you as you are working on writing and getting your book published.

Student: I just wanted to confirm; you have to get permission to quote from a Bible?

Answer: Yes, Bibles are copyrighted materials. As I said earlier, I quoted from the *"Dake's Annotated Reference Bible"* and I had to get permission to use the quotes. Because the *"Dake's Annotated Reference Bible"* is not my work, I had to go to the Dake's publishing house to get their permission. God's Word in the published Bibles did not just show up dangling in the air but someone took the pain and money to publish and release it to the general public. Although the Word of God in the Bible is free to the public (**Public Domain**), but the *Finis Jennings Dake's* published version is not in the public Domain. Mr. Dake made his version of the Bible very unique in his published edition by adding commentaries and references that enabled him to copyright the version. Therefore, you need permission to quote from his version of the Bible if you are going to make full reference to his version of the Bible.

But, if on the other hand you said in your book, the Bible said… and you did not reference a particular version such as *"Dake's Annotated Reference Bible,"* you may not run into copyright issues because the Word of God in the Bible is in the public domain. But, the minute you cite the *"Dake's Annotated Reference Bible"* or use any of his commentaries, you then need to ask for permission to use the reference.

Books in the Public Domain

Things in the public domain are free for public use. They are not protected by the laws of usage such as copyright or patent laws. Therefore, books that are in the public domain are books that are not protected by copyrights or patent laws. They are books that the public can freely use without violating copyright laws.

In publishing, books that are in the public domain are books that can be quoted from freely because the copyrights on them have expired. As of now, according to copyright laws, all the books **published** prior to 1924 are now in the public domain! This means that you can quote from any of them without copyright infringement. For example, some people have taken books that were published in the 1800s and added their own commentaries to them and republished them with copyright protection on the new versions of books. In other words, they customized the books and republished them under their names while still affirming the original author, but they have the copyright to the new book. You can also freely use the work of the original authors but if you choose to cite the republished version with commentaries, you will run into copyright laws concerning the new version.

It is worth noting here that **unpublished works** (manuscripts) are not covered by the copyright expiration dates because they are under the federal copyright law for the life time of the author plus 70 additional years after that!

I have talked a lot about the works of *Flavius Josephus* that have been republished by several different authors but the original works by *Josephus* himself are forever in the public domain. Old books are republished all the time by people that want to put their own two cents in or who just want to reintroduce the books to the public. **As a serious writer, you want your readers to be able to reference the materials that you cite in your book and if you use a book that has no reference in print today, your readers may never be able to locate the work, so it might be necessary for you to quote from a republished version that contains the original work.** This way, the people who read your book might be able to get a copy of the reference if they need to.

For example, if I quote from any of *Flavius Josephus'* works and all I say in the bibliography is *Josephus* without telling the readers where to get the materials, I have not done them any justice because I did not tell them where to get the information. Therefore, they will begin to wonder if the materials from *Josephus* are verifiable. As a result, I cannot just say for instance, "*The Jewish Wars*" by *Josephus* period. I have to give the reader enough information to help him or her locate the materials. The internet is now making the referencing of old books easier.

If I was to add my commentaries and footnotes to any of *Josephus'* work and customize the book and republish it under today's copyright laws, you would have to get permission from me to use my copyrighted version. As I stated before, you can freely quote the original work of *Josephus* without any permission because his work is in the public domain but how can someone find *Josephus'* printed materials if you do not give them any reference? For instance, if I were to tell you to go buy *Josephus'* book, you would ask me what the title was and who the publisher was. *Josephus* does not have a publisher today but so many people have taken his work and customized it and republished it under their names while still giving *Josephus* credit for the work. Today, it is easier to find *Josephus'* works in republished books. I had to get permission to quote from the republished books even though I was still talking about *Josephus*.

So far, I have published twelve books and all my books are copyrighted to me. You will find that at the end of each of my books, I give the reader information on how to locate any book that I quoted from. I get permission when I use quotes from other people's books. By the same token, if someone is going to quote from any of my books, they had better come get permission from me because they are all copyright protected.

Student: How about the dictionary? Do you have to get permission to quote from the dictionary also?

Answer: Yes. Dictionaries are copyrighted materials also. There are different types and versions of the dictionary out there. Take for instance, the Webster's Dictionary. I found out that Webster's Dictionary has several types and editions. There is the regular *Webster's*, the *Webster's II, Webster's Collegiate, Webster's American Family, Webster's New World, Random House Webster's, Merriam-Webster's*, etc. It was like a nightmare but I finally found the Webster's company that owned the copyright to the edition that I quoted from.

My quotes were from the *Webster's II New Riverside University Dictionary* published in 1984 and the company told me that this particular edition of the Webster's Dictionary was out of print! They informed me that what they have now is the *Webster's II College Dictionary* and **they wanted my reference to reflect this edition instead of the old one.** They gave me the exact words that they wanted me to use in my bibliography page.

This is another point that I had not mentioned before so I will tell you now that some publishing houses or companies might tell you in writing exactly how they want the reference to their book to appear on your bibliography page. They care about how you present their company and the quoted materials.

The rule is to make sure that you know the rightful copyright owner of the version or edition of the dictionary that you quoted from. As I stated before, companies are bought and sold all the time so do your homework about ownership early in your writing stage.

Student: Can we use people's actual names when writing about something that they have done? Can they sue because their names were used?

Answer: It is always a good thing to change the actual names of the people in your book to protect the guilty and the innocent. You may not be sued as long as you are not running around quoting people's real names.

Student: Do they still have a legal right to sue you when you do not mention their real names?

Answer: Anyone can sue anyone for any reason but they will have to prove that you are not referring to another person. Most writers avoid law suits by using fictitious names in their works. For example, the inside of my Visions and Dreams book (**Keys to Understanding Your Visions and Dreams**) and my Spiritual Discernment book (**How to Discern and Expel Evil Spirits**) are questions from the students who took those classes. Some of the students gave me permission to use their real names. But for the others, I had to change all their names to protect them. Not only to protect them but to protect me because we can be smiling today but things can be very different tomorrow. I did not want a future law suit. The following is how I indicate that the names of the people in the book have been changed:

> *Note: The names of some of the individuals in this book have been changed to protect their identity. Any coincidence with the real name of any one in the general public is not intentional.*

How many of you remember some years ago when a very popular singer's dad sued her? Yes, her own father sued her. Therefore, you cannot assume that because someone is your friend today, they will always be on your side. Suppose the friendship breaks down tomorrow and the person says, "I know how I can get back at you, I'll just sue you to get money for some of the things you did while we were friends?" You will see the so-called former friend on TV crying as he or she narrates how the former friend did him or her wrong or took advantage of him or her.

In the case of a group of people, they can all claim that they did not really know what they were doing and that they were railroaded. They will cry on TV and make you look bad publicly. Therefore, it is good to always change the actual names of people in order to protect their identity. Unless someone has given you written permission to use his or her real name, you are to make sure that you do not use people's real names in your book.

Always remember that some people have a very good legal mind or they might know someone who could give them counsel on legal matters. Such people might know the legal implication of your using their real names in your book. Therefore, they might choose to come after you financially when your book turns out to be a best seller. They might sue you for an amount that is greater than what you made from the sale of your book. This is how it works sometimes so be sure that you do not use people's real names without permission.

Student: How do you handle writing a book about one's personal life such as a book about my life and the abuse that I went through? How should I handle my ex-husband? I mean using his name?

Answer: Your case is unique because even if you say my ex-husband, people that know the two of you will know exactly who you are talking about but still, in order to protect yourself from a law suit, you have to tell your story without direct reference to his name. This is where legal counsel comes in because it involves serious legal consequences. You need the guidance of an attorney. Have you only been married once?

Student: Twice.

Answer: Twice? Even if you have been married twice and you say one of my ex-husbands, those who know you and your ex-husbands will know who you are talking about but if you have proof of the abuse like police reports, medical records, sworn testimonies by witnesses, etc., then you can safely tell the history of the abuse because you have documents that can prove your case in a law suit. **Still, I will advice you to consult with an attorney before you publish your book with your ex-husbands' names on them.**

Also, if you can tell your story without using the actual names, do. You could say "one of my abusers" as a way of getting around using the actual name. **You have to find a synonym that is good and that will protect you from possible lawsuits but the best thing to do will be to have an attorney take a look at the manuscript to determine if you are safe to use the names that you choose.** There are people out there looking for someone to sue in order to make money and some ex-husbands have sued their ex-wives and vice versa. Therefore, you have to make sure that you protect yourself from lawsuits.

Obtaining Book Reviews

The process of obtaining "book reviews" is similar to that of obtaining an author's permission. Book reviews are written comments by the people who have read your manuscript. They are usually very favorable to you because they are written by people who are in support of what you have written. When you pick up a book, you will usually see reviews that tell you that the book is a very good book or that it is a book that you should read in order to gain some insight into the subject the book is addressing.

Just like obtaining permission to quote from someone's published work, you have to contact the person you want to write the review for you. From experience, I have found that when I put in a request for someone to review my book, I really have to work on getting them to sit down and write the review and to send it back to me. By work I mean, send follow-up emails, phone calls, reminder letters, etc., to make sure that the person has not forgotten about my request.

The truth is that when you ask someone to write a book review for you, what you are asking the person to do is to <u>sit down</u> and <u>write</u>. For some people, this can be tedious especially if they do not like to write. We tend to judge people by what they have, their position in society or their accomplishments and we forget about their areas of weaknesses. You might see some people walking about as though they have everything all put together in their lives, have all the fame or money they need and they enjoy a prominent position but sitting down to construct grammatically correct sentences might be something they find intimidating or tedious. Therefore, never assume that everyone you ask a review from is a writer.

Purposes of Book Reviews

The basic truth is that book reviews are used to sell your book. They are meant to encourage the reader to buy your book. For example, **To His Glory Publishing Company** places book reviews not just on the back cover of the books that we publish, but also on the second page of the book after the title page. The reason is because reviews are advertisements to help authors promote their books. When someone picks up a book, we want to let the person know that someone else feels that the book is good. We want to let the person know that someone said that the book is "a must read."

Therefore, book reviews tell the potential book buyer that someone other than the author has read the book and their comments declare the book to be very intriguing, life changing, an eye opener, etc. Some book reviews advise every reader to make sure that they have the book in their collection of books or in their possession. The reviews will encourage the potential buyer not to put the book back on the shelf but to go ahead and buy the book. Book reviews are therefore marketing tools.

Obtaining a Foreword for Your Book

A foreword is something that you use to also promote your book. It does the same thing as book reviews; especially if the person who wrote the foreword is a well known public figure or an internationally acclaimed authority on the subject or topic that you wrote about. For instance, some of our authors have received forewords from nationally and internationally acclaimed Christian ministers.

When you get a foreword from a very well known person, potential book buyers are encouraged by the foreword to go ahead and buy your book because the well known public figure testifies that the book is good. What we as publishers do is display the popular person's name on the book cover to show that the person approved that the book is good. It makes some people feel comfortable that a popular person has read the book and the endorsement convinces them that the book is good.

Therefore, the bigger the name that you can get to write your foreword, the more some people may be convinced to buy it. Also, if the person has a ministry tool that can help promote your book, approach the person to see if he or she can help you market your book through their ministry tools. You may want to do this because if the person was willing to put his or her name out there for you, the person may also be willing to help you promote or advertise your book to the audience that he or she has influence over.

I encourage you to make sure that you get a foreword and make sure that you get reviews for your book whenever possible. As I said before, just like obtaining copyright permission, they can take a long time to get if you do not handle the process well.

Reviews and forewords are different from permissions because as you saw in my previous discussion about obtaining permissions, you can actually expedite the process by sending a Permission Request Form and a Permission Granted Form. But with a foreword or review, you cannot tell the person what to write about your book. It has to be their genuine assessment of your writing.

Always remember that the person writing your review or foreword has the sole discretion to decide what to say about your book. All you can do is to basically bug them with emails and phone calls until they get back to you with the review or foreword. If you ask someone to review your book or write a foreword for your book and you do not hear from the person, do not assume that they do not like your book.

What I have discovered is that there are some prominent people out there that when you ask them for a review or a foreword would not get back to you because you are not a well known public figure. If they think that you are a "no name person" (not known nationally), they are not going to respond to your request. You just have to learn to navigate around such people when you encounter them. Never let them make you feel small.

Warning about Responses to Your Request

Just as in the case of a permission request, be prepared for a NO response. Besides the people that will not reply or acknowledge your request for a review or a foreword, some might get back to you saying that they do not give reviews or forewords. You have to be prepared to handle such a response and not get discouraged.

One of the set backs that I discovered about getting someone to write a review or a foreword, is that we tend to send the person our entire manuscript. What this does is create a major reading project for the person. I learned from experience that it is usually not necessary to send the person your entire manuscript initially. The bigger your manuscript, the more time the person feels would be needed to read it. This alone can make it difficult for them to both read and write a review or a foreword. If time is of no essence to you, then you can give a person your entire manuscript and wait for the person to get back to you when he or she has had the time to read it all.

I learned to have mercy on people by giving them the synopsis of my topic; the outline of the work, the major chapters that show my perspective on the subject, the table of contents and the conclusion. An outline of the main chapters will help them to see how the book ties together to the end. You can then tell the person that you will be glad to send them the entire manuscript if that is their desire.

Always remember that this process is different from trying to get someone to edit your book. You may need to send the person your entire manuscript but as much as possible, try not to create a major reading project for those you are asking for quick reviews and forewords. Instead, make your book a summary outline or a note outline but give them what they need in order to get the full gist of what your book is all about. Sometimes, it may require that you give them the whole manuscript but you let them decide.

The goal is to give them what they can easily read so that they can give you a review quickly. If the manuscript you give them is too big, it might take them a whole year to get through reading it before they can get back to you. Some might put the manuscript aside until they go on vacation because that is when they think they will have the time to read it. The problem is, suppose they do not go on vacation? Suppose they forget about your manuscript when they are ready to go on vacation? The truth is that people do not have time to read large manuscripts, so make it easier on them by giving them only the necessary portions of your manuscript.

The following is what happened when I wanted a foreword from a prominent Christian minister in Chicago and I sent him my entire manuscript. I was all excited after speaking with his Administrative Assistant and she told me to email the manuscript and that she would give it to him. I downloaded the entire manuscript to her but when I called the next day to see if she had received it, she was very displeased with me. She said to me, "Your book tied up our computer for a whole day because it was one hundred and something pages long!"

It appears that they had a very slow computer and receiving a large manuscript that tied up their computer had ticked her and the rest of the staff off. She rudely asked me if I have ever considered the minister's travel schedule and ministering time. She was still angry as she informed me that the minister was way too busy to sit down and read a hundred and something pages of my manuscript! I never heard from them to this day.

This is one of the reasons why I advise you to make sure that you do not overwhelm the person from whom you are asking a review or a foreword, with a large manuscript. As I said before, do not create a reading assignment for them before they can write a review or a foreword. Just give them the information that you think they need in order to effectively write a review or a foreword. Always let them know that you will be more than willing to send them the entire manuscript if they need it.

Only Send Out Edited Materials for Reviews

I knew a writer that was trying to be cheap because he did not want to spend money to have his book professionally edited. After reviewing the manuscript, I told him that it needed editing but he did not want to hear it. He told me that one of his friends had already edited the manuscript and I told him that it was not well edited and he went away in defiance.

About a couple of months later, he took his manuscript to someone to read in order to give him a review but the person basically drove him away saying that he could not read the manuscript because it was too poorly written and that he needed to have it edited! The person practically told him that he was not willing to put his name on a book that was so poorly written. When the writer came back to me, I had to basically rewrite every sentence in that book before it was suitable to hand out to anyone for a review.

A Word about Your Reviews

The size of your book will determine how many reviews can be displayed on its back cover. Therefore, not all the reviews that you get are going to be used by your publisher. If you want your book on Amazon.com for instance, it has to be at least 5 x 8 and this size of book has room for no more than a couple of reviews. One of the things that I do when I get back reviews from people is to prepare them so that their feelings are not hurt if their reviews are not used.

You, as a new writer also need to prepare those who

give you reviews by informing them that their reviews might or might not be used. If you do not prepare them, they might be expecting their names to be on the back cover of your book and some of them might be very disappointed if their reviews are not used.

    Therefore, it is good to let them know as they give you the reviews that the publisher will only use the most appropriate reviews. It is best to tell your best friend that the publisher might not use his or her review so that you do not jeopardize your relationship. Reviews are meant to help sell your book so only the reviews that will best help sell the books are used.

Chapter 4

Positioning Your Book for Marketing

The size of your book is very important because many people do not like to purchase large books. Therefore, do not scare off the potential book buyer with a large book that is about the size of an encyclopedia or a dictionary. Learn to market your book effectively by applying the following techniques so that when it appears on the market your book might become a best seller.

1. Have Multiple Volumes
Rather than have a giant book that no one wants to pick up and read because it is too big, create multiple volumes of the same book. Let each volume address different aspects of your subject or topic. For example, my prayer book has two volumes and I have two more volumes that I need to publish in order to complete the set. I had to break them into volumes because I know that modern day book readers do not like large books.

Breaking them up into volumes enables me to market the books without intimidating the buyers with one large book. Each volume addresses different prayers. There is no prayer that is duplicated in either one of the volumes and people love both volumes. Although, I was just trying to manage the size of the book when I started out, I discovered that there was an added financial benefit to having the book in different volumes. It became a blessing for me to have several volumes that address different prayer needs.

I could have combined them and produced one big book that no one really wants to pick up because of its size, but I thought about several volumes and being in the publishing business, I came out with the first two volumes. Volume one is priced at $16.95 while volume two is priced at $18.95. Even from a financial point of view, if I had combined the two, how much do you think I could have asked the public to pay? A generous amount would probably be $19.95.

By default, I came out ahead financially because I can now sell each volume separately. I could have given it all away in one large book that nobody wants to buy. I say to you therefore, that you should begin to think about splitting up your manuscript into volumes when it becomes too big. Publish it in two volumes and then price them in a way that you can be reasonably compensated for your work. As I said, I have prayers outlined up to volume 4 of my **Effective Prayer for Various Situations** book series and when I have the time, I am going to begin writing out the prayers in volume 3 and volume 4 so that I can also release them.

As you can see, one idea for a book can actually generate multiple sources of income for you if you know how to effectively market your book. Many people do not think of multiple volumes or setting up multiple sources of income when they are writing a book. They put all their ideas in one big book and they tote it around like a dictionary or an encyclopedia. They truly expect other people to carry around their big book. Do not become one of them so break up your large book into volumes.

It might cost you money to publish each volume but as the sales go on for a long period of time, you are going to get more back financially because people buy the book in two volumes. For example, instead of pricing one large book at $19.95, you can sell each volume at $19.95. Therefore, breaking up your book into two volumes captures the sales benefits from two volumes and you come out ahead financially. I have discovered that when people like volume one of your book, they will immediately buy volume two when it is published.

The volume one of my prayer book was so well received and in high demand that when volume two came out, people were already aware of the nature of the book and bought it as well.

2. Create Manuals

Another way that you can strategically market the materials in your book is by creating a manual that can be used along with the book. If you know me, you will know that I like to create manuals to be used along with some of my books. For instance, if you have been to my **Visions and Dreams Class**, you will notice that each student has a manual and a book. I did the same with the books for my **Spiritual Discernment Class** and my **Mentoring Class**. Each of the classroom books has a manual that the students can use to follow along with my teaching in class. Now, as a writer, do you not think that I was smart to have created manuals that students can use to follow along my teaching? Over the years, I have seen them become a great source of additional revenue as well as help the students get the most out of the class.

With proper marketing, manuals can become additional sources of revenue along with your book. The following is what I said at my first Writers' Conference as I gave each attendee a handout that was an excerpt from this book on publishing. I had to give the excerpt to them free of charge because this book was not yet published. After I gave it to them I said, "What I just did was give you all a part of my upcoming manual on publishing for free because it is not yet published. I am working on the actual manual and book and they are not yet finished; so you are blessed to get them free of charge. By the time I get done with my writing and they are published, you will be purchasing the manual along with the book that teaches you how to write and publish your book. The manual is meant for you to use to follow along my teaching because the information that I am teaching is right there in the manual!" Doing this I believe was wisdom and an effective marketing strategy.

I have also created a journal to go with the Visions and Dreams books and another one to go with the Spiritual Discernment books. You just have to know how to market what God has given you because He meant for it to be a source of blessing to you. Every once in a while, we run a promotion on the book sets and give discounts or free journals.

3. Create CDs and DVDs

As I stated above, you have to know how to market what God has given you. I have found out that there are people who do not like to read books. They prefer CDs and DVDs, so I make sure that there are also CDs to go with some of my books. These are CDs that contain my teachings on the topics in my book.

If you are not called to teach, you can have someone read your book and create a CD so you can market it on a CD. You have to make sure that it is done professionally because you want to produce a CD or a DVD that is well done and sounds good.

Note: *Remember that the materials in this book were first presented in a classroom and conference setting. As a result, some of the chapters have question and answer sessions at the end.*

Questions and Answers about Marketing

Student: Will you be my marketing manager?

Answer: Really funny. Oh yes, if you can pay me. But on a serious note, we do have a book distribution service here at **To His Glory Publishing Company.** It is an additional service after publishing.

Student: How did you learn about sales and marketing?

Answer: When I was growing up in Africa, one of the things that I had to do was learn how to make a quick sale and I thank God for helping me to do it. My grandmother made homemade food, household soap for sale along with produce such as mangoes, oranges, cashew fruits, etc., that I had to go out and sell after school. Some days, I went with some people to their farms to pluck the fruits before I could sell them but I learned that I had to quickly turn around and sell my produce before it became bad.

I learned the value of quick sales and effective marketing very early. Initially, once I came back from school, I would eat and immediately go out to sell whatever I had to sell that day. I spent a great part of my afternoons and evenings selling things.

All that changed when one day, I was going around selling and at about 5 p.m. I came by the King's Palace and I saw the King sitting with some of his counselors. They were enjoying the cool evening breeze. On that day, I was selling "plantain pudding" and I immediately went to them and told them that my grandmother made the best "plantain pudding" and that I was offering them the best pudding in town. To me, I was trying to make a sale but to the King, it was a good opportunity for him to talk to me again about his cocoa plantation. My friends and I would go to his cocoa plantation and eat the cocoa fruits and throw away the seeds.

Because cocoa seeds are used to make chocolate, cocoa plantations were not to be play grounds for children but we freely played and ate the cocoa fruits without saving the seeds beside the trees as we were supposed to. As a result, we were brought before the king and warned by him not to throw away the cocoa seeds. The King told us that it was OK for us to eat the fruits but we were to put all the seeds back into the cocoa pods and place the pods beside the tree. We never obeyed the instructions because we still threw away the seeds and his youngest son would sometimes come to chase us around in the plantation. We all loved the chase because we could all outrun him. It was usually a perfect opportunity for us to practice our fence jumping while he was in pursuit of us.

On that day, the King wanted to have another word with me and he promised to buy all my plantain puddings if I promised not to throw his cocoa seeds away but first he wanted to know if I had personally eaten the pudding. I had a reputation of being a child who did not like any type of food no matter how well it was prepared and I was vocal about my dislikes. One of the things that I liked was my grandmother's plantain pudding. I told him that I had truly tasted it and that it was good and he bought everything that I had to sell! To me, a great marketing strategy was born. I learned that selling in bulk and mass marketing was better than hawking my goods from house to house.

As a result, I noted the time that the King and his counselors came out every evening to enjoy the cool evening breeze and whenever I had something to sell, I went up to them with whatever I had and they bought them all. From then on, when I came home from school, I ate and I played while waiting for the King and his counselors to come out in the evening. At about four thirty, I was off to the palace to sell. If the King was out of town, I would go around town looking for places where people were gathered together so that I could make the most sales in one stop. I stopped going about town looking for one-on-one sales because I had learned that it was better to reach the most people at one stop. It was my own little introduction to mass marketing! Therefore, I developed a new strategy of looking for where people were sitting around having conversations or where people were sitting around enjoying the evening breeze while playing a board game and I would make all my sales there.

Sometimes, they would buy everything that I brought

just so I would go away and not come back to bother them that day. It was truly in those days that I learned the value of strategic marketing. I learned how to make the most sales with just enough efforts. Therefore, when I began to publish books, I had to think about how I could best produce and market my products so that the people were blessed and so that I was also blessed.

Using the same sales strategy that I developed in my early childhood days, I was quick to realize that in publishing, people do not like to read big books. Therefore, I utilized a strategy of breaking up my large prayer book into several volumes so that I could maximize my book sales.

This strategy worked because Volume 1 that I priced at $16.95 went all over the world and people call us from different countries wanting the book. The marketing side of me again noted that, since the book was in high demand, why not notch the price of Volume 2 up a bit. I made the second volume a little bigger and I priced it $18.95! Again, I say this to let you know that you have to learn how to use what God has given to you as a source of financial blessing.

Student: With manuals or books that the people send to your publishing company; can you publish a spiral bound?

Answer: Yes, but some spiral bound books cannot readily be displayed on the online bookstores. We can do it here at **To His Glory Publishing Company** but it will require a different book setup. You will have to discuss the particular setup that will be available to you with the publishing house that you choose.

Student: Have you read some of the ex-presidents' biographies? Some of them are like a dictionary?

Answer: They can do that because for one thing, they have dedicated followers. People are curious to read about how a person made it to the position of a president. They also hope that the ex-presidents will clear up some scandals concerning themselves and their administrations. They have a large audience in their political parties and many people enjoy reading their books. Their books are usually bestsellers.

Also, there are some books that the general public is very familiar with and they will not mind a large volume of it. The key is to first be well known and people will buy your book even if it is large. Take for instance the person that wrote the Harry Potter series; do you know how many millions she gets paid to write a book? She can make it as big as she wants or as small as she wants because there is a market for it already. The first Harry Potter book that got the people hooked on the series might or might not have been that much of a big book, but as it began to produce followers and buyers, she probably sat down and said, "You know what, I just got me a jackpot. I am dishing it out they are licking it up." Now, she can choose to make her book as big or as small as she wants because there is a huge market for it.

Once you have created a market for yourself, you can do whatever you want because you are a proven author in that area and people know and trust you. They know what to expect from your books. For example, the textbooks and the manuals that I use in my teaching sessions are medium sized and I sell them as sets. They are usually required classroom materials for my classes or workshops. Now that many people are beginning to know about my books and my ministry, I do not have to worry so much about the size of my books but I prefer to still keep them medium size.

Chapter 5

Basic Rules About Choosing Your Topic

Collecting Your Thoughts

The topic or subject you choose to write about can make your book relevant or irrelevant. In other words, people might or might not be interested in your book depending on the topic that you choose to write about. Therefore, before choosing a topic, make sure that it is one that will appeal to the general public.

It is necessary for you to really think about the topic you want to write about because many people have submitted manuscripts to our publishing company that were mostly their biographies without any appeal whatsoever to anyone except their family members. This is not to say that writing a biography is not to be encouraged but rather, to let the would-be writer know that biographies are harder to sell to the general public when the writer is not a famous person or a very well known public person.

Others have not only submitted their biographies but they have no concrete topic to make their biographies relevant to anyone else. Many of them have had publishers reject their manuscripts because they did not see a market for what they submitted in their writings. Therefore, I advise those who write their biographies to make sure that they tie them to topics that are of relevance to the general public or a segment of the society that they have targeted to reach.

Research Your Chosen Topic

Once you have chosen a topic to write on, you need to conduct a research of the topic in order to see what has been written about it. You need to know the prevailing belief about the topic by the general public so that you can see how your thoughts can either help to advance the belief, bring a new perspective to the belief or help change the belief if it is wrong. It will help you to assess how the public may react to your chosen point of view.

Also, researching your topic will help to broaden your perspective about your chosen topic. You need to know the current reference materials on your chosen topic. Knowing what has already been written about the topic will help to prepare you so that you are better able to defend your chosen position on the topic. This is critical if you are writing a scholarly work or one that might have two opposing positions or different schools of thoughts.

Be sure to use the library and the internet to research your chosen topic. There are libraries in just about every city in this country so make use of them. Also, the internet is a good source of reference materials and you can buy books on Amazon.com, Barnesandnoble.com and other online bookstores. The internet has now made it easy to obtain reference materials on many topics. Therefore, take advantage of the opportunity and ease of research that it represents.

Have a Unique Perspective on Your Chosen Topic

Determine early in your writing process the unique perspective or revelation that your book will give the reader. As I have just stated, reference materials will show you what the prevailing view point is on your chosen topic so that you can learn how to present your view point or argument. Your goal is to make sure that what you are trying to write about is actually needed by the general public. Your book should add something to what is out there in other books and if you think that what is already out there is wrong and you have a new perspective that is going to help, then let your unique perspective be well articulated in your book.

Getting the Attention of the Potential Book Buyer

Your job is to convince the potential book buyer in the bookstore to buy your book rather than the other books. This means that the title of your book and the colors you choose for the cover should move the potential buyer towards your book. The writing on the back cover and the preface/introduction page should also stir the potential buyer to desire to read your book further and as a result, buy the book. Your job as a writer is to engage the attention of the reader so that he or she will not want to put down your book.

For example, if you were to pick up my very first book titled, **"Unveiling the God-Mother,"** you would discover that it is very difficult to put it down once you have started reading it. The reason is because it engages you and I deliberately wrote it that way. Although I am the author, when I received the first copy of the book from the publisher, I said, "OK, let me review this book " but to my amazement, I sat up all night reading it without putting it down! A lot of times, people say to me, "When I picked up your book, I just had to keep reading it because I could not put it down. I had to finish the book because I wanted to find out what happened next in every chapter."

Not only do you want to get the attention of the buyer at the bookstore, you also want them to choose to read your book at home. When they pick up your book, you do not want them to put it down and go read some popular author's book just because the author is well known. You want your book to have something to offer to the reader in his or her reading time at home. This is why you define the reason for writing and you define the audience that you are writing for. You do this by asking yourself the basic questions in writing: Who, what, when, where and how. You also determine how you are going to best reach the people and you can use the preface page or the back cover write-up to do this.

Writing About Secular Subjects

We have published poetry books, medical books, health books, real estate books, school books, and novels by different professionals like flight attendants, real estate brokers, medical doctors, etc. You can write about whatever you want to write about because we, at **To His Glory Publishing Company,** do not assign topics to authors. However, we do not accept manuscripts that are anti-Christ, pornographic, obscene and profane because we are a Christian publishing company.

Because nobody wants to read a book with inaccurate information, make sure that the information you present in your book is current and accurate on the subject. If you are going to tackle a secular subject, make sure that you are well informed about the subject and that you can adequately defend your position on the subject. Also, be prepared to answer those who have opposing view points on the subject because some of them might be very passionate about it.

Many Christians think that you cannot write a book on a secular topic. If you decide to tackle a topic that a lot of people have already dealt with, then know that you will deal with issues such as the placement of your book on Amazon.com online book listings. For example, if the title of your book has been used by many other authors, your book might end up being number fifty or sixty on Amazon.com book listing. People will have to scroll through a lot of pages before they can find your book on the online bookstores like Amazon.com.

Therefore, make sure that you choose a book title that is unique and can be displayed on the first page. It is better to follow the same requirements as the government's requirements for setting up a corporation. You need to do a title search on Amazon.com and Barnesandnoble.com to see what position your selected title would likely be in.

Selecting Your Title

The title of your book can either kill or sell your book. By this I mean that your book title can either move a potential buyer towards your book or away from your book. The title of your book is your "extra, extra read all about it" promotional statement. I always tell writers to imagine a book buyer standing in a bookstore with many books to choose from and to ask themselves the question; why should the potential buyer take a step towards my book instead of the others? The reason for this question is because the buyer is faced with so many book titles and only the title that offers a significant benefit will have the most appeal to the buyer.

Take for instance the title of this book, **"Secrets about Writing and Publishing Your Book,"** I chose this title because my target audiences are <u>those who want to write a book</u>, <u>those who are writing a book</u> and <u>those who will also want to publish their book once it is written</u>. I immediately let the potential book buyer know that this book is a "how to" book. I let him or her know that this book offers help in areas of writing and in how to get published. Book titles carry a lot of weight and writers have to know how to effectively use the title of their books to sell them.

Yes, the right book title can help you sell your book. As a result, you need to research your chosen book title in order to make sure that it is not already exhausted by other writers. **Book titles are not covered by copyright laws;** only the book contents are covered by copyright laws. Therefore, there are many books with the same book titles already out there in the market. Your book can have the exact same book title as other books but a problem arises when people are looking for your book on Amazon.com, Barnesandnoble.com or local bookstore. As I stated before, if you choose a popular book title, then, those who are looking for your book on the online bookstores will have to scroll through many pages before they can see the picture of your book.

You want your book title to be unique enough to be displayed on the first page of Amazon.com or barnesandnoble.com when a potential book buyer keys in the title. Usually, books are displayed on online bookstores first in alphabetical order and then by publication date. Therefore, you do not want your book title to be buried as number 25, 50, or 100 of books with the same title.

The Importance of Colors

The colors and images on your book cover can also help to market your book. If you have a dull book cover, people might not find your book appealing even if the contents are good. The fact is that some books are forgettable. In other words, there are books that you can walk by without even giving them a second look. People pass by forgettable books without even noticing them because the colors are dull and the title is not appealing or catching. The book title and the color or images in the cover do not draw people towards the book. Therefore, when designing your book cover, you need to seriously think about the colors that are going to appeal to the general public and the title that will best inform the reader what your book is about. Choose colors that standout and draw the attention of those who look at the book. Do not let your book blend into the bookstore background.

For instance, if you look at the title of my newest book titled, **"Understanding the Power of COVENANTS,"** you cannot just walk by and pretend that this book is not appealing to you because the colors are vibrant colors, the title is inviting and the images are clean cut. It is supposed to draw your attention and you cannot miss the way the word **COVENANTS** is boldly displayed on the title.

If you bought the very first edition of this book, you will notice that the book cover has changed. The original title was **"UNDERSTANDING THE POWER OF COVENANTS"** and it was spread out over three lines. Doing this made the title too wordy and too top heavy. In my opinion, it was unappealing so we decided to shrink the letters down to small case letters except the word covenants. It made a huge difference in the beauty and appeal of the book and we decided to play up the word Covenants. In the first edition, the word was just buried among the other words but in this second edition, the word **COVENANTS** stands out conspicuously. Anyone interested in the topic will move towards the book in the bookstore.

Some people do not think of marketing when it comes to the title they select for their books. Some authors have come to us with very long titles that they said they got from the Lord. Who am I to say that the Lord did not give them the title when they said that He did? Therefore, we do not tamper with such titles since they got it from the Lord. Such titles to me are tamper proof.

Note: *My word of caution here is; make sure that you truly got your book title from the Lord before using it. Do not enforce your wishful desires on your publisher because your book title, images, and colors in your book cover will help to sell your book.*

When it comes to grammar, I have had to tell some people that God does not speak bad English when they insist on no editing because it is the word of the Lord. I tell them that God is infallible and as a result, His English is perfect and we must therefore transmit what we receive from Him with the correct grammar that He spoke to us.

Dr. Mary J. Ogenaarekhua

Questions and Answers about Color and Artwork

Student: Can the author suggest the colors of the book?

Answer: You can suggest the colors that you want but if your suggested colors do not work, we will let you know. Some ideas sound good until you create a book cover. If the cover does not look good with the colors suggested, then the author has to be willing to try other colors. This is where you have to work closely with your publisher but if an author insists on a particular color, we will give the author the colors that he or she wants. After all, the author is the owner of the book. We always aim to please the author but we also want the general public to be pleased with the output.

Nevertheless, authors need to be aware of things that are associated with certain colors, images or symbols. For example, if you are talking about heaven or heavenly beings, there are certain colors that people associate with heaven and heavenly beings. Things like white clouds, blue skies, a dove and angels. Therefore, you have to make sure that your ideas do not create an image association problem for the book buyer.

Also, when you are talking about purity for instance, there are certain colors that you might want to consider and restrict your choices to because you want the cover to also give the impression of what your book is about. These are some of the things that you need to think about when selecting the colors and images or symbols for your book cover.

Student: Can people give you artwork to use for their book cover?

Answer: Yes. A lot of people have given us artwork to

use in creating their book covers. Some have even had a graphic artist draw an image for them and they gave us the image to use in creating their book covers. For instance, if you should look at my book that is titled, **"How to Discern and Expel Evil Spirits,"** you will see that we used a dove on the book cover. The reason is because people already know that a dove speaks of the Holy Spirit and that the sky and the clouds speak of heaven.

Our suggestion is to let your book cover, book title and the colors that you choose help the reader understand your topic or subject. In other words, make them relevant to what the book is about. For example, we had an author who wrote about interpersonal relationships. In essence, his book was about what you need to know so that people do not make you become discouraged in life because of repeated disappointments. To make his book title relevant, we suggested a subtitle and a visual image that shows a setting for good interpersonal relationships.

Because he has many adopted children, we suggested that he go with his family on a picnic and take several pictures that show them in a happy setting. He took his entire family on a picnic and took pictures of all of them on a sail boat depicting a happy setting. He sent us some of the photographs of the picnic and we used one of them to create a beautiful book cover for his book. When you look at the cover, you can really see a very happy relationship displayed in the picture.

Student: I can truly see how your book cover can help sell your book by telling the reader what your book is about. This is really good information for me. How about if you are writing a biography?

Answer: You can still use the same principle of letting your book cover tell your story. There was another author whose manuscript was about how God delivered him from three consecutive prison life sentences. While in prison, he prayed to God and God brought him out. According to him, the publishing houses that he initially contacted did not want to publish the book but we accepted the manuscript because it was a great testimony of the grace and goodness of God. He brought the manuscript and we saw immediately why it had been rejected because it needed extensive editing.

He has since become an associate pastor and we needed to let the book cover tell his story. We told him to go have his picture taken by a professional photographer. He had some pictures taken and we selected one of the pictures and the graphic designer created a book cover that showed a before and after picture of his life story. We had a very imposing picture of him with the background showing a criminal on the run! It is a very powerful book cover that lets the reader know that the author has gone through a process of transformation.

Sometimes your title and your book cover can tell a story of the saving grace of God which is what this author's book was about. You might come to us with an idea but we are willing to sit down with you to brainstorm about the book cover once we have read the book. Our goal is to give you ideas that will best help to tell your story and to sell your book at the same time.

Student: Can someone just submit a concept about a book cover?

Answer: Yes, but the most difficult book covers are the ones when the author gives you a concept. A lot of our book covers are from the concepts that our authors submit it to us. It is fun and it allows creative gifts to flow in our graphics department. The only pitfall about creating someone's concept in general is that it is very time consuming and if the person is difficult to work with, it can become tedious. We actually have had a couple of authors who were difficult to work with because they could not admit that their concepts did not work on paper. Also, you have people that cannot make up their mind and they solicit counsel from all their friends and as a result, change their concept every time you turn around.

Doing this can be costly because unless the concept was not what you requested, you cannot just blow off hours or days of work by the graphics people. Therefore, know what you want and be flexible to ideas that might enhance your book presentation. Creating a book cover requires the publisher and the author working together in a professional and pleasant manner. It should be a fun process.

Chapter 6

Your Book Size, Layout, and Formatting

Book Size

In publishing, the size of your book matters. We have had people inform us that they have a book that they want to publish. They get all excited and we make an appointment for them to come into the office and they pull out fifteen or twenty pages of manuscript and they truly believe that it is a book! Below are some of the things that you need to be cognizant of as you are writing your book.

Pocket Size Books

You can write a pamphlet or a mini-book but for full publishing, you need a real book. This means that you need at least fifty pages of manuscript in a Word Document and on an 8.5"x 11" paper. When you size down fifty pages of an 8.5"x 11" manuscript, you get at least one hundred plus pages to make a pocket size book. We refer to 5"x 8" books as pocket size books.

A person once came to our office with twelve pages and she seriously believed that she had written a book for adults and that the book would be a best seller! My thoughts as I was watching her were; if twelve pages make a book, then everyone should be a published author. You have to make sure that you have enough pages for at least a pocket size book.

The reason for the fifty-page requirement is because it gives your book a fairly decent spine to write your name and the book title on. The spine is what people see when your book is on the shelf, so it is a great place to advertise your book.

Pocket size books (5"x 8") are the fastest selling books because the reader is not intimidated by the size. They do not come across as reading projects that a reader might want to avoid. The next best size is the 5.5"x 8.5" size. A person does not mind buying a big dictionary or an encyclopedia because they are reference books where you look things up but when it comes to reading a book, people want a book that they can easily finish.

About Large Size Books

A pocket size book is the easiest size to sell because if you look at society today, you will see that it is not a book reading society anymore. Older people are the ones reading books these days while a large portion of the younger generation spend their time on their play stations, computer games, sending and receiving text messages on their blackberries etc. We have to face the fact that we are dealing with a TV/Video generation that is not interested in large size books. If you give them a huge size book to read, they will not read it because it is too much of a reading project for them.

Having a large size book will work against you as an author because people are not quick to purchase large books anymore. For instance, if someone is standing in a bookstore trying to buy a book and the person likes your book, they might decide to wait until they have enough time to devote to reading it because it is a big book. The person might decide to come back and buy it when he or she is going on vacation. The question you ask yourself therefore is; when the person is ready to go on vacation, will he or she come back to that bookstore again? Will he or she remember your book? Chances are that the person will not. Therefore, my advice is that you should not let the size of your book make you lose sales.

My Observation at a Book Sale Table

I recently went to a book table to observe book sales after a public speaker had finished delivering his message. I watched as his 5"x 8" and 5.5" x 8.5" books were being sold at a fast pace but I noticed that his book that looked almost like a dictionary in size was not even being looked at by the buyers! Why was no one looking at the book? I believed that the reason was because it was too big. When you looked at it, all it said to you was, lots of reading time needed for this book. I watched as people just moved away from it to the other smaller books. People move towards the smaller books because they believe they can be sitting in the doctor's office and finish it or they can pick it up and finish reading it in a couple of nights.

As I said before, you want to make sure that your manuscript does not become too big and that you do not end up with a large size book that people are not eager to buy. I always tell new writers to start to wind their manuscript down once they reach eighty to ninety pages. Your book will not become too big if you limit your manuscript to be between 100 and 125 pages. A 100-125 page manuscript will give you a medium size book.

Book Layout

We provide you with a professional book layout and by book layout we mean, taking your manuscript from an 8.5"x 11" document and reducing it to the size that is most appropriate for your book based on the total number of pages of your manuscript. We also make sure that it is laid out professionally, has equal margins on all four sides of every page and looks appealing.

Here at **To His Glory Publishing Company,** we will layout your book in a way that makes it very attractive and appealing to the eye of the reader. I do not like to pick up a book and see a sloppy layout work. I do not like to fight with a book while trying to read the text on the left side that is too close to the spine.

Most publishing houses require that you submit your manuscript to them in an 8.5" x 11" Word document and most prefer the Book Antiqua 12 point font. They will then edit the document and lay it out in the size they think will best help sell the book. There are other book sizes such as 6" x 9', 7"x 10", 8.5" x 11," etc. One way that we try to make a book not appear too big or too thick is to bump it up to the next size, use smaller font size, condense the writing, etc.

Again, publishers determine the size of a book based on the number of pages they receive from the author. For instance, if you give us a manuscript that runs between 60 and 85 pages, chances are that your book will be a 5"x 8" book (small size) because if we lay it out on the next size which is 5.5 x 8.5," it will look too tiny or too flimsy. Therefore, using the 5" x 8" book size makes it look like a fairly good size book and gives the book a nice spine.

The size also helps determine how much you can charge for the book. An author's book might not sell very well if the author wants people to pay twenty dollars for a small size paperback book. Maybe someone who loves the author and the author's immediate family members might be willing to pay twenty dollars for such a little book, but the general rule is that you want people to feel that they are getting a fair deal when they are buying your book. In other words, you want them to feel that they are getting their money's worth.

There are some small books that sell for an exorbitant amount because they are for some highly specialized professions or trades, but in general, small books are not priced very high. Paperback books are known not to cost as much as hardback books. You have to always keep this in mind when it comes to setting the price for your book.

As you can see, the size of the manuscript that you give your publisher will determine the size that they make your book and it will also determine how much they can fairly or reasonably ask people to pay for it.

Creating a Fair Size Book

Sometimes, we help authors who do not have quite enough pages to create a decent size book. Every publishing house can do this but it may increase the cost of publishing your book. For instance, if you give us a manuscript that is only forty pages, we may have to make it double space in order to give you more pages because we do not want your book to be too small. Another reason publishers require at least fifty pages of manuscript is because, for your book to be displayed on the online bookstores, it has to be at least a certain number of pages. As I said before, one of the smallest book dimensions that we can display on online bookstores is the 5 x 8 size.

Therefore, a forty page manuscript is not quite enough to make a decent size book that can be displayed so we can help the author out by using the following options. Double space the entire manuscript, make the margins larger on every page, add more pages to the manuscript, etc. Depending on what we are trying to accomplish, we can either add pages to your manuscript or reduce the number of pages that you give us.

Book Formatting

Most publishers prefer that you do not format your own manuscript before you submit it to them. **To His Glory Publishing Company** also prefers that you do not format. We strictly do not want you to format. One of the reasons is because professional publishing software is customized to handle the layout of books differently from the software on most personal computers. There are specific software that most publishing houses are required to use when they submit books to their major distributors for printing.

Some software do not always readily interpret formatting from other software programs the same way. For example, text boxes and pictures inserted into a Microsoft Word document often relocate to other areas of the document when downloaded into professional publishing software.

Also, if you have on the Tracking function in Word, even if you turned it off before uploading the document, some publishing software can still create problems when you upload your document. Therefore, when you give your publisher a regular Microsoft Word document that has been edited and has very basic formatting, it does not create any problems.

Paperback vs. Hardback Books

It is an author's choice whether to make a book a paperback or a hardback. I personally prefer the paperback because they are easier to carry from place to place. With hardback books, you may have a duster jacket to cover the hardback and it is hard enough to deal with the hardback because it makes the book too cumbersome to carry about and to add a duster jacket to it does not help matters.

The duster jacket becomes a pain because you cannot take it along with the book as it tends to rip. Once you remove it from the book, you have to hunt it down when you are done reading the book because you do not remember where you put the jacket. Another thing is that books with duster jackets tend to be dull once you remove the duster jacket because the hardback cover is a basic plain color and they tend to only have the title of the book and the author's name. This is one of the reasons that my books are usually paperback books because I want to make it easy for people to take them from one place to another without them being too cumbersome.

Another reason I make my books paperback books is because they are less expensive when it comes to publishing. A hardback book is more expensive than the paperback one when you are given the estimated cost of publishing and printing your book by your publisher. Also, you will continue to spend more than the cost of a paperback when you need more copies printed. Yes, the initial choice you make between a paperback and a hardback book is going to affect the cost of publishing and reprinting copies of your book.

Using Images inside Your Book

The inside of your book is called the book interior and you can choose to use pictures, artwork or any type of graphic inside your book. First, you must make sure that you have the legal right to use any image from another book, encyclopedia, newspaper, magazine, etc.

Secondly, you want to make sure that the images you submit to your publisher are very clear with high resolutions. We ask for images, tables, charts, artworks, illustrations, etc, with at least 300 dpi. A lot of the images that you find at online search sites have very low resolutions such as 70 or 90 dpi. Therefore, they do not yield a good resolution when used in a book. A very good resolution yields beautiful and readable artwork and images.

Using the Proper Tab Key

You will not have the proper or true spacing in your document if you just use the space bar instead of the tab key to make indentations for your paragraphs. You must use the proper tab key to set your indentations for every paragraph before submitting your manuscript to your publisher. Using the proper tab key will ensure that the spacing in your document is not lost and that the spacing is consistent throughout your document when it is downloaded into the publishing software.

Using the Bold Key

If you want some things bolded in your book, go ahead and bold them in your Word document. For instance, we prefer that you bold all your Bible scriptures and put them in quotation marks. When using parenthesis to show a scripture reference, be careful to make sure that you place the period after the parenthesis. You do not want the reference in parenthesis hanging unattached to the information. Here is an example of what I am talking about.

> **"The thief cometh not, but for to steal, and to kill, and to destroy; I am come that they might have life, and that they might have it more abundantly"** (John 10:10).

If you notice, the period or full stop is after the parenthesis. Also, if you use a semicolon, do not let the semicolon hang outside of the quotes. Many writers do this because they have forgotten the basic rules of grammar. This is why I have included two chapters in this book that deal with the basic rules of grammar and the basic use of punctuation marks. I hope that they will serve as a refresher for those that want to brush up on their grammar so that they can become effective writers.

I use bolded materials to make my books beautiful on the inside because it helps the eyes of the reader. It gives the reader's eye a break because people's eyes can easily become tired after reading one very long paragraph after another without a break. If you look at my books, you will see that where there is a scripture quote as in the example above, the scripture is bolded and indented on both sides. I do this in my books to give visual appeal and to give variety to the text to help reader's eyes.

Chapter 7

The Art of Writing

Ghost Writing

As I stated in the preface, writing is an art and nothing will happen until you are willing and disciplined enough to put your thoughts down on paper or on a computer. You will eventually need to sit down and write your book unless you have the money to employ a "ghost writer." Employing a "ghost writer" means paying someone to write your book for you so that you do not have to sit down to write the book yourself. If you choose to go this route, you will need to give the person the outline of the topic and subjects that you wish the book to address or a recorded cassette or CD that the person can transcribe and write the book from. A lot of wealthy people choose to write their books this way.

The purpose of using a ghost writer is to spare those who are too busy to write, too lazy or have no writing skills the actual "pain" of writing. It is the easiest way to become an author without actually writing. It has its place in publishing but for those who want to write their own book or cannot afford the services of a "ghost writer," the art of writing can be learned. I personally wrote all my books because I enjoy writing.

Writing as an Art

Some people defeat themselves when it comes to writing because they are convinced that they do not have what it takes to become an author. The dictionary defines an art as **a system of principles and methods used in performing sets of activities** such as a trade or a craft. **The truth is that methods can be learned and so writing as an art can be**

learned. I have a lot of respect for those who have disciplined themselves enough to put their thoughts down on paper and to have it published. It is an effort worth commending.

No one is ever too old to learn to write when the person's faculties are functioning as they should. As I have already said in the preface, **published books can still be around hundreds of years after you are gone! People can still find out about your thoughts and ideology as they read the topics that you write about.** Therefore, you should try to learn the art of writing or discipline yourself to write down the topic that has been tugging away at your heart.

I personally believe that the worst failure in life is the failure to try. As a result, I do not allow fear or past failures to prevent me from moving ahead to do what is burning in my heart that I know God has placed in there. If you have been afraid or worried that your command of the English language or your background is not good enough to warrant you to be an author, then, this book is for you. It is time for you to rise up and overcome those fears because the rules of English grammar can be learned.

Chapter 9 of this book deals solely with the <u>**Basic Rules of English Grammar**</u> **that you need to know in order to write a mature manuscript**. It is my hope and desire that after you have thoroughly reviewed these rules, you will overcome any fear or lack of understanding that you may have been dealing with concerning writing.

You may not be able to change your past but you sure can change your future by refusing to live in the defeats of yesterday or yesteryears.

Writing with a Purpose
You have to clearly state what the purpose of your book

is or let the reader know what your book is about. This means that you have to let the reader know the main subject of your topic (the **who,** the **what,** the **where,** and the **when)**. The reader does not have to spend a great deal of time reading your book and not be able to tell what the book is supposed to be all about. I said before that a lot of people write manuscripts that we consider as being "nothing about nothing." This means that the manuscripts have no clear purpose, there is no real topic identified and the entire manuscript is just a collection of all types of experiences and discussions that are not made relevant to the reader.

In order to write with a purpose, you need to think through what it is that you want the general public to know. This means that you have to know from the get go that you are writing for other people to read and not for yourself alone. Actually, writing is for others and not for the writer.

The rule is to know that it is not about you but about the reader understanding what you are saying. Your book should motivate the reader and create some passion or excitement in him or her as she reads it. If you choose to write a "how to" book, then, it should let the reader know that it is a book that will help the reader know how to do whatever it is that you want them to learn. At the end, it should provoke or guide the reader as he or she steps forward to accomplish the goal.

As a new writer, you have to set a reasonable goal of what you want to accomplish with your book and you have to make sure that you stay within your stated goal so that you do not go off on rabbit trails as you try to move the reader from one paragraph or chapter to another.

Have a Book Outline

Once you have chosen your topic, done your research and formulated your thoughts on the topic, an outline will help you address the relevant subjects within your topic and it will help you to stay on point. It will help you to organize your subjects in their order of importance or relevance and it will help you to organize how you want to advance your thoughts or point of view on the topic. You can build up your arguments to a point of climax before you begin to offer solutions or changes.

An outline will help you write in a concise manner. Without an outline, your writing might go off to irrelevant topics or subjects that would end up making your book seem to lack a specific purpose. What you need to bear in mind is that an outline basically helps you to get a handle on your writing.

Chapter 8

Understanding the Parts of Your Book

Inside your book are key parts that are common to well published books and they are the **book spine**, the **title page**, the **endorsement page, publisher's page** which is also known as the **book vein**, the **acknowledgment page**, the **dedication page**, the **table of contents page**, the **chapter pages**, the **conclusion page** and the **bibliography page**. Let us take a quick look at each of them.

The Book Spine

The book spine is the edge of the book that you see when you stand it on a book case shelf. It allows the publisher to display your name and the title of your book so that even if the book is on the shelf, a person can still read the spine to get the necessary information about the book. It is also the reason we require that your book be at least fifty pages because if the book is too small, then it will not have a spine wide enough for the publisher to write on. The spine of your book helps to advertise your book by providing a place to write the necessary information for the readers to see.

The Title Page

This is the first page of the inside of your book and it restates the title of the book because in case someone cannot read the small print on the spine, they can clearly see the title on the first page. It helps to imprint the title on the mind of the reader so that they are not likely to forget it.

The Endorsement Page

This is the review page that shows the comments and reviews of those who have read the book. It is meant to encourage people to buy your book. It is a promotional page. An example of an endorsement from one of my books, (**How to Discern and Expel Evil Spirits**) is shown below:

> *"Never have I seen a more comprehensive teaching on the origin of evil spirits and how to cast them out. God has given Prophetess Mary a powerful gift of discernment but better yet, a gift to teach what she understands from the Word of God! The book* **'How to Discern and Expel Evil Spirits'** *is an incredible teaching tool. Prophetess Mary's insight on recognizing demon spirits and how to deal with them can equip the saints for spiritual warfare. I especially love the chapters on the Origin of Evil Spirits and Can a Christian Have a Demon?"*
> -**Dr. Aaron Motley, Pastor**
> **Miracle Deliverance Temple of Christ,**
> **Montgomery, Alabama.**

As you can see, it is the genuine view point of someone who has read your book. It shows what the person thinks and it a good promotional tool.

The Publisher Page

This page is called the vein or life line of your book because it contains the author and the publisher's contact information for those who are interested in purchasing the book or contacting the author. Without this page, people will not be able to contact you or your publisher and as a result, will not be able to get a copy of the book. This is the reason it is called the vein, because it carries the life line of your book.

Without the contact information on this page, your

book is dead because no one will be able to get a copy of it. When the vein contains the appropriate information, anyone anywhere in the world can contact you or your publisher concerning the book. Here, at **To His Glory Publishing Company**, we usually provide our authors with this page and most other publishers do the same.

The Dedication Page

This is the page that you use to dedicate the book to all those who you want to honor with the book as you mention their names. You can dedicate your book to God, to your father and your mother, to your children, to your friends, to your special loved one and whoever you want to dedicate it to. It is different from the acknowledgement page.

The Acknowledgement Page

This is the page in which you thank or acknowledge all those who have helped you concerning the book. You can thank all those who encouraged you to write, who helped you financially, who typed the manuscript and who edited the book. You can also thank your family members for being there for you during your writing process.

The Foreword Page

This is the page that displays the commentary of someone who has read your book and has a bankable name. By this I mean, someone who is either well known, famous or rich enough to help sway the general public to view your book favorably. For example, if someone writes a book on real estate and the person gets Donald Trump to write a foreword for the book, many people will want to read the book because Mr. Trump is well respected in the Real Estate business. Again, the foreword page is also a promotional tool.

The Introduction or Preface page

This page allows you to briefly inform the reader of what the book is all about without giving away the entire plot. This is where you give the reader a brief synopsis of the book. If you give away the plot, then, there is no need for someone to go any further to read the book. Instead, you give enough information to whet the reader's appetite and to inspire him or her to want to read the book further. Make either your preface page or your introduction page brief.

Some people use the introduction page while others use a preface page. Either one is OK. Some authors might choose to only use the foreword page and not include a preface page or an introduction page.

The Table of Contents Page(s)

Your book should also have a table of contents page. Sometimes it is one page but you can have more than one page. I have started to do something a little bit different with the table of contents page of my books. I now display both the titles and the subtitles in each chapter in my table of contents page so that I can give the reader a preview of what the book contains.

In effect, I am simply using it to advertise the book to the potential buyer because as a person is going through the table of contents listing, I want the person to get excited and buy the book. As the person is looking at all of the topics listed on the table of content page or pages, my goal is to get the person to decide that he or she needs a copy of the book. You have to use the tools within your book to advertise it as much as possible.

It could have been easy for me to just list the main chapter titles in the book in the table of contents page but if I did only that, I would have lost the opportunity to further advertise the book to the person looking at it. But by listing every single title and subtitle in a chapter, I am telling the reader that these are topics that he or she should take the time to read about. The message to the reader is: take the time to read this book. Buy this book because the titles and the subtitles tell you what it has in store for you. To me, the table of contents page has become a very good marketing tool.

The Chapters in Your Book

It is helpful to have the main subjects of your book divided into chapters. You can then deal with each subject extensively. You should let the subjects flow from one chapter to another. This means that you should arrange your subject in order of importance. You should arrange related subjects close together in your book chapters. The goal is to build up your view point or build up your argument to a climax in your book. You should use each chapter to accomplish this goal.

The Conclusion Page(s)

The conclusion section of your book should not be so large that it is another major section of the book because as the reader is approaching the conclusion section, he or she is thinking about the book coming to an end. Therefore, do not make it a tedious experience by going on and on about the topic that you have already addressed in the book. Your conclusion can be half a page or it can be a page but do not make it more than two pages. It should be a brief summary of your book and the final words that you want to leave the reader with.

In other words, your conclusion should be a summary of the main points that you wrote about in your book and your final appeal to the reader to either shift his or her way of thinking about the issues you addressed or make a life style change. You are basically expressing your hope that what you wrote about had a positive effect on the reader.

The conclusion section allows you to prescribe whatever course of action you want the reader to take. For instance, if you addressed people that are overcoming addictions in their lives, then in your conclusion, you want to encourage them to take the first step towards getting free of their additions. It allows you to say the last words that you have for your readers.

The Bibliography Page(s)

The bibliography page of your book is basically a place for you to give credit to the authors, publishing houses, magazines, etc., for the materials that you quoted or cited. Use your local library to find out the correct way to display bibliographical information about the author, the publishing houses, year of publication, page number, etc. For instance, the author's last name comes first and it is followed by a comma. Next, you have the author's first name which is followed by a period or full stop.

The Advertisement Page(s)

Besides the normal publisher page (vein) in your book, some publishers like to advertise some other books on the last page or pages of all the books that they publish. Therefore, you can sometimes see other people's books advertised in your book just as they will also advertise your book in other authors' books. You have to be aware of this practice so that you do not appear to be difficult when other writers' books are advertised in the last page or pages of your book.

Here at **To His Glory Publishing Company**, we include a page of some of the books that we are advertising but we are flexible enough to accommodate authors who do not want other people's books advertised in the last page of their books. When an author says NO to us including this page in his or her book, we make sure that it is not included.

Bookstore Order Form

We do something that is unique with the very last page of all our books. We include a **Bookstore Order Form**. The reason we do this is because some people might immediately want to order a copy of your book or have a bookstore near them carry the book as soon as they come across it. Therefore, we make sure that we include an order form in the back of all of our books which can be used to order our books. Any person or any bookstore can use this form to order any of our books from anywhere. They do not have to call the author or contact anyone else because they can just mail the order form directly to us.

We have discovered that this form is a very useful tool in selling books. It helps us and it helps our distributors to make sure any bookstore can have access to the book when they need to. The author does not have to worry about designing this form because we include the form in all the books we publish.

Chapter 9

Summary of the Basic Rules of Grammar

This section of the book is intended to give the reader a basic summary of some aspects of **English Grammar** so that he or she is better prepared to write a manuscript that is grammatically correct and comprehensible to all those who will read it. I have discovered from many of the manuscripts that we have received that a lot of writers and would-be-authors do not have a basic understanding of the English language when it comes to writing.

There is a great difference between conversational English and written English. Most would-be-authors are not aware of this because many of them write the way that they speak! They lack the knowledge of the basic rules of grammar. It is my hope that the following will help the reader acquire a basic understanding of the English language in order to produce a well written manuscript.

Parts of Speech
The Eight Parts of Speech are:

1. <u>Nouns</u>
   They are the names of people, places, and things. Some ideas can also be used as nouns. They tell us something about the **who** and the **what** in a sentence. Examples of nouns are: **John** (a person), **Atlanta** (a place), **a chair** (a thing), **philosophy** (an idea), etc.

   Examples of nouns:
   John is a man. The name John is the noun in this sentence.
   Atlanta is a city in the State of Georgia. The name

Atlanta is the noun in this sentence.
Philosophy is a field of study. The word philosophy is the noun in this sentence.

2. <u>Pronouns</u>
   We substitute pronouns for nouns. They tell us who or what. They are used in place of the name of a person, place, thing or idea.

   Examples of pronouns:
   I, you, he, she, we, they and **it**.

3. <u>Verbs</u>
   They tell about the **action of the noun or pronoun.**

   Example of a verb:
   Mary <u>is</u> reading. The action word in the sentence is the verb **is**.

4. <u>Adverbs</u>
   They tell us about **how the verb acts**.

   Examples of adverbs:
   John **gently** sat down. The adverb in this sentence is **gently**.
   He considered the proposal **carefully**. The adverb in this sentence is **carefully**.

5. <u>Adjectives</u>
   They help us to know **how the noun appears or looks**. They are words like **large, small, beautiful, skillful**, etc.

   Examples of adjectives:
   Janice is truly a **beautiful** lady. The adjective in this sentence is **beautiful**.
   John is holding a **small** book. The adjective in this sentence is **small**.

6. **Prepositions**
They are used to connect words. They are words like **at, in, on, to, into, on top of,** etc.

Examples of prepositions:
John is **at** home. The preposition in this sentence is **at**. The book is **on top of** the table. The preposition in this sentence is **on top of**.

7. **Conjunctions**
They are also used to connect words. Conjunctions are words like **and, but, or,** etc.

Examples of conjunctions:
Read the Bible everyday **and** you will know the ways of God. The conjunction in this sentence is **and**.
They looked all over the city **but** they did not find the dog. The conjunction in this sentence is **but**.

8. **Interjections**
They are sudden interruptive words or phrases used as exclamations.

Examples of interjections:
Wow!, bravo!, way to go!, etc.

Let us look at the parts of speech in more detail beginning with nouns.

Nouns

Nouns are names of persons, places, things or ideas. Examples: **Mary, Atlanta, chairs, science.**

Types of Nouns
- **Common Nouns**   Example: **Church**
- **Concrete Nouns**   Example: **Pizza**
- **Abstract Nouns**   Example: **Joy**

☐ **Collective Nouns**   Example: **Team**
☐ **Compound Nouns**   Examples: **Ice cream, Mary and Martha**

Nouns can be singular or plural. **Examples:** Shoe vs. Shoe**s**; Friend vs. Friend**s.**

When nouns end with the following, **s, x, z, sh** and **ch**, their plural is formed by adding **es**.

> **Examples:**
> The singular Class *becomes the plural* Class**es**.
> The singular Fox *becomes the plural* Fox**es**.
> The singular Quiz *becomes the plural* Quizz**es**.
> The singular Dish *becomes the plural* Dish**es**.
> The singular Sandwich *becomes the plural* Sandwich**es**.

When nouns end with **f** or **fe**, their plural is formed by making the **f** or **fe** a **v** and then adding **es**.

> **Examples:**
> The singular Thie**f** *becomes the plural* Thie**ves**.
> The singular Lea**f** *becomes the plural* Lea**ves**.
> The singular Wi**fe** *becomes the plural* Wi**ves**.

When nouns end with **y**, you form their plural by adding **ies** in place of the **y**.

> **Examples:**
> The singular Compan**y** *becomes the plural* Compan**ies**.
> The singular Famil**y** *becomes the plural* Famil**ies**.

Noun suffixes are what you add to a **root word** (the main part of a word) in order to give it a different meaning. They can be additions such as **ance, er, ness**, etc.

Examples:
When you add a suffix to Perform, it becomes Perform**ance** or perform**er**.
When you add a suffix to friendly, it becomes friendli**er** or friendli**ness**.

Possessive Nouns They show the ownership of a noun. You can use an apostrophe (') with an **s** when the noun is singular (**'s**).

Example:
Mary's book.

When the plural form of the noun ends with an <u>s</u>, you can use an apostrophe <u>without</u> adding an <u>s</u>.

Example:
Writers' workshop.

If you want to avoid apostrophe, you can use **of** or **for** instead of an apostrophe.

Example:
<u>Writers'</u> workshop becomes workshop **of** writers or workshop **for** writers.

Nouns and Sentences
When a noun is connected to a verb, it becomes the subject of a sentence. A subject and a verb can form a sentence.

Example:
Mary runs. <u>Mary</u> is the **subject** and the verb is <u>runs</u>.

Objects

Most times we add another <u>noun</u> to a <u>subject</u> and a <u>verb</u> and we call it an <u>object</u>. A noun + a verb + object = Complete

Sentence. Therefore, most sentences consist of subjects, verbs and objects.

> **Example:**
> Mary has a book. <u>Mary</u> is the noun, <u>has</u> is the verb and <u>a book</u> is the object (an additional noun).

Subject and Verb Agreement
In English grammar, your subject, verb and object have to be in agreement in tense, numbers, quantities, amount, etc.

> **Examples of subject and verb tense agreement:**
> **I** study (singular).
> **You** study (singular).
> **He or she** studies (singular).
> **They** study (plural).
> **We** study (plural).

You cannot say **we studies**. The proper tense when using **we** in this case is **study**. When using the past tense, you then say: We **studied**. Your subject and verbs must always agree.

Subject and Object Agreement
Also, your subject and object must agree.

> **Example:**
> **Five students** came to the class and **they all had books.**

Since there is more than one student (subject), we must use plural **books** (plural object) instead of a singular **book**.

Identifying the Subject in a Sentence
To identify the subject of a sentence, you place the word **who** before the verb.

> **Example:**
> <u>Mary left the room.</u>

To help us find the subject, we place **who** before the verb **left**. **Who** left the room? The answer is **Mary** (the subject).

To identify the Object of a Sentence
To identify the object of a sentence, you place the word **what** after the verb.

> Example:
> Let us still use the same sentence <u>Mary left the room</u> as our main sentence.

To help us find the object, we place **what** after the verb <u>left</u>. Mary left **what**? The answer is **the room** (the object).

Pronouns

They are substitutes for nouns. We use them to replace people's names, places or things.

> Examples:
> **I, you, he she, we, they** and **it**. They can be used to ask a question. **Who, what, where,** etc.

Adjectives can also be used to point to a specific person, place or thing.

> Examples:
> **This one, that one** or **those ones.**

The only pronoun that refers only to an inanimate object is **it**. We do not use **it** to refer or address people.

The Use of Person in Grammar
We need to understand the use of person in grammar. By this I mean, the use of **first, second** and **third** person.

> **First person**= the person speaking.

Example:
I am warning you.

Second person=the person you are speaking to.

Example:
You have been warned.

Third person= the person or thing spoken about.

Example:
He has been warned.

The following are examples of the use of person with the pronoun **it** (inanimate subject pronoun) to show possession of an object.

Examples:
1st Person = **It is mine.**
2nd Person = **It is yours.**
3rd Person = **It is hers.**

When constructing a sentence, it makes a great difference if we choose to use first, second or third person. Using a lot of third person sentences instead of first can make your manuscript seem very impersonal, tedious to read and boring. The most effective and powerful sentences are the ones written in first person. To demonstrate this, look at the following sentences again.

1st Person = **I am warning you** (very powerful).
2nd Person = **You have been warned** (less powerful).
3rd Person = **He has been warned** (least powerful).

You can see very clearly from the above sentences that the most powerful of the three sentences is the first person sentence. You can also see that the most impersonal and least powerful of the three sentences is the third person sentence. Therefore, I advise the would-be writers to minimize the use of third person sentences in their manuscript. Use it only when it is necessary.

Singular and Plural Forms of Person
The following are the singular and plural forms of 1st, 2nd and 3rd person.

> **Examples:**
> 1st person singular = **I, you, he, she** and **it**.
> 2nd person plural = **We, you,** and **they**.
> 3rd person singular = **He, she** and **it**.

Note: Depending on how it is used, **you** can be singular or plural. Also, **they** can be used to denote people or inanimate objects. The gender pronouns are: **He, she** and **it**.

Ownership Pronouns
The ownership pronouns are **mine, yours, his, hers, its** and **ours**. They show ownership, possession or relationship to a person or a thing.

Note: An apostrophe is used with possessive nouns but not with possessive pronouns.

> **Examples:**
> Possessive noun= It is Mary**'s**.
> Possessive pronouns = It is **mine**, it is **his**, it is **hers**.

You cannot say it is mine's.

Object Pronouns
The object pronouns are **me, you, him, her** and **it**.

Verbs

They tell us what the noun or the pronoun does, owns or

is experiencing. They show action, being or a state of being.

Types of Verbs
1. **Action Verbs.** These verbs tell us the action in a sentence.

    Examples:
    I **dance**, I **sleep**.

Dance and sleep are the action verbs. Some of them might have a preposition before them.

    Examples:
    to dance, to get, to sleep, to go, etc.

    Example:
    I like **to dance**.

2. **Non-action Verbs.** These verbs tell us about the condition of a person's frame of mind or a person's senses.

    Examples:
    I **understand**, I **think**, she **looks**, etc.

3. **Linking Verbs.** These verbs link the subject of a sentence with a specific word that either describes or renames the subject.

    Examples:
    Janice is a **swimmer**, Jane is a **Nun**, Craig is a **Pastor**, etc.

4. **Helping Verbs.** These are verbs that help the main verb in a sentence to convey its full meaning. The verb "to be" is one of the primary verbs in these sets of verbs. It shows a state of being.

    For example, the verb <u>to be</u> is conjugated as follows:
    I **am**

You **are**
He/she **is**
He/she/it **was**
We **were**
They **are**
They **were**

There are other examples of these types of helping verbs such as **to do, to have** as well as special helping verbs like **could, would** and **must**.

Forms of Verbs

Verbs change into two forms and these forms are known as regular form or irregular form.

1. **Regular Verbs.** These have patterns that are predictable when they change forms.

    The following is an example of how the **verb dance** changes form:
    I **dance** at home
    I **am dancing** at home
    I **danced** at home
    I **have danced** at home every week

As you can see, the form of this verb is very predictable as it changes from present, present continuous, past and past participle in the sentences.

2. **Irregular Verbs.** They have an unpredictable pattern when they change form.

    Examples:
    He **eats**
    He is **eating**
    He **ate**
    He has **eaten**

Verb Tenses

Use the appropriate verb tenses in your writing because wrong verb tenses will result in a bad manuscript. Therefore, study verbs and their tenses.

> **Example of Verb Tenses:**
> **Present tense** = I **exercise** everyday
> **Present continuous** = I am **exercising**
> **Past tense** = I **exercised** yesterday
> **Present perfect** = I **have exercised** several times
> **Future tense** = I **will exercise** tomorrow.

The Participle Parts of a Verb

There are four principle parts of a verb. Below are <u>the four participle parts</u> of the verb **to go**. These are the stages of your participation in an activity.

> **Examples:**
> Luke **goes** to school = **Base Form or Root Form**
> Luke **went** to school = **Past Participle**
> Luke **is going** to school = **Present Participle**
> Luke **has gone** to school = **Past Perfect Participle**

The above forms are the main forms that most verbs change into. Therefore, you need to pay close attention to the form that you choose when constructing a sentence. In other words, use the appropriate form that will correctly express the action of the verb.

I have discovered that a lot of writers do not pay attention to the part of the verb that they choose in their sentence structures. Therefore, I want you to be mindful of these parts of a verb so that you are not one of the writers that I am talking about. Know how to correctly use the root or base form, the past form, the present participle and the past participle of the verb you choose.

Adverbs

Adverbs are words used to describe verbs, adjectives or other adverbs. They are used with verbs, adjectives or other adverbs in order to give them a broader meaning. Most adverbs are formed by adding **ly** to an **adjective.** Examples of adverbs are words such as **gently, carefully, quickly, rudely, slowly,** etc. It is not all adverbs that end in **ly**. Some of the adverbs that do not end in **ly** are: **already, far, almost, afterwards, back, where, more, low, fast, next, so, long, too, then, still,** etc.

Types of Adverbs
1. **Adverbs of Time.** They are words such as **today, now, soon, tomorrow, before,** etc.

   Example:
   I came back from New York <u>today</u>.

2. **Adverbs of Degree.** They are words such as **almost, nearly, very, completely,** etc.

   Example:
   He <u>almost</u> forgot the book.

3. **Adverbs of Manner.** They are words such as **quickly, slowly, abruptly,** etc.

   Example:
   Janice <u>quickly</u> left the room.

4. **Adverbs of Location.** They are words such as **inside, above, below, there, here,** etc.

   Example:
   A policeman is <u>inside</u> the building.

5. **Adverbs of Frequency.** They are words such as **often, sometime, always, never,** etc.

Example:
I <u>often</u> read at bedtime.

Every writer needs to learn how to use adverbs correctly because they enrich your writing skills. Note the difference between an adjective and an adverb.

Examples:
She dances **skillfully** (adverb).
She is a **skillful** dancer (adjective).

One of the quickest ways to identify an adverb is by asking the question **when, where** and **how.**

Adjectives

They help us know how the noun looks or they tell us about the quality of the noun or pronoun. They make the nature of the noun clearer and in so doing, limit the meaning of the noun or pronoun. Some of them describe the color, size, shape, etc, of the noun or pronoun. They are words such as, **red, small, ugly, beautiful, this, my, your, whose, any,** etc.

Example:
Jan is <u>beautiful</u>. The adjective is **beautiful.**

Some <u>adjectives help us to determine</u> the noun instead of describing it.

Example:
<u>Your African friend,</u> Ama is the one who left the note.

Other adjectives show us ownership.
Example:
It is <u>my</u> book.

There are adjectives that are demonstrative. They are: **This, that, those,** etc.

Examples:
That boy is intelligent.
This girl is nice.
Those are the people next door.

Some adjectives are numerical because they show us quantity by stating the numbers.

Example:
One of the boys took the book.

Prepositions

They are words that come before a noun or a pronoun in order to show relationship between them and a location, a direction or a movement. Some frequently used prepositions are: **at, in, on, to, into, on top of, out of,** etc. They help us to understand time, location, direction and movement.

Examples of the use of prepositions in sentences:
1. The bell rang **at** 2p.m. *(it shows time)*.
2. The book is **on top of** the table. *(it shows location)*.
3. James walked **into** the room *(it shows movement or direction)*.
4. Janice was sent **out of** the room. *(it shows movement or direction)*.

Learn to use prepositions in your sentence structure because they help to clarify what you are saying by pointing out the exact movement, direction, location or time of the events or ideas that you are trying to communicate.

Prepositional Phrases

When a preposition is before a noun or a pronoun, it is called a prepositional phrase. The reason is because the noun or pronoun becomes the object of the preposition. Therefore, all prepositional phrases have their objects in a sentence structure.

As a writer, you must make sure that all your prepositional phrases have their object. It will help to make your manuscript grammatically correct.

Example:
On the kitchen table is a loaf of bread.
On the kitchen table is the prepositional phrase. The object is **a loaf of bread.**

Conjunctions

They are used to connect words or groups of words in order to show how they are related. Conjunctions are used to join words or groups of words together. They are words such as **and, but, or,** etc. They are words that indicate an addition to a sentence. The three types of conjunctions are:

1. **Coordinating Conjunctions**
   They are used to link words and they are words such as **but, for, and, so, yet, or,** etc.

   Examples:
   I believe John's story **but** I still have questions about his character. The word **but** is the coordinating conjunction.
   Look for someone to cheer up **and** you will forget your own troubles.
   Drink a glass of orange juice everyday **and** you will greatly improve your health. The word **and** is the conjunction in these sentences.

2. **Correlative Conjunctions**
These groups of conjunctions are used in pairs. They are words such as **either ...or, not only ...but also, whether ... or, neither... nor,** etc.

Examples:
I believe that **either** James **or** Helen will win the race.
Not only was he late to the meeting, but he was **also** rude about it.

3. **Subordinate Conjunctions.** They are used to link an independent clause with a dependent clause. **Examples of subordinate conjunctions are as, as if, as long as, as soon as, because, after, before, if, since, whenever, wherever, though,** etc.

Example:
He walked into the meeting room **as if** he owned the company.

Conjunctions are very good tools in creating a sentence because they help the writer produce a mature and well written manuscript.

Interjections

They show strong emotion, sudden and interrupting words or phrases such as **Oh!, Wow!, Ah!, Hey!,** etc.

Examples:
Oh! I forgot my bathing suit in Janice's car.
Hey! Do not worry about it.
Ah! There you are at last!

Clauses

These are words that contain subject and verb that

can express a complete thought or can be used to complete another part of the sentence. They enrich your writing by allowing you to add details that will help you to express your exact thought or meaning.

Clauses are either **dependent** or **independent**. The following is an example of an independent and a dependent clause in the same sentence.

Because Julia Roberts earns over $17 million dollars per movie, *(dependent clause)* **she is considered one of Hollywood's highest paid actresses** *(independent clause)*.

Independent Clause
These are clauses that can express complete thoughts on their own or they can communicate an idea on their own. They are complete sentences that can stand alone without additional information. They are called the main clauses. From the above sentence, we can see that the second clause can stand alone as a complete sentence.

She is considered one of Hollywood's highest paid actresses.

The second clause above fully expresses the idea that the writer is trying to communicate in the latter part of the sentence. The reason is because it is an independent clause. Because it clearly and fully expresses the idea being communicated, it is independent and you can put a period or a full stop at the end of it.

Dependent Clauses
They are used in a sentence to modify another clause. They do not fully express or fully communicate an idea on their own. They are called dependent or subordinate clauses because they are sentence fragments. They require additional information for them to make sense.

Example:
Because Julia Roberts earns over $17 million dollars per movie

Due to the fact that the word **because** began this clause above, it is not able to stand alone. More information is needed to complete the idea being expressed in the clause. As a result, you cannot end the sentence with a period or full stop. You need to add the missing information before people can understand what you are trying to tell them about Julia Roberts.

Chapter 10

Use of Punctuation Marks

Consult some materials on grammar so that you can learn about the rules of punctuations. You will be surprised to learn about the number of people that do not know what to do with colons, semi colons, commas, quotes, brackets, double quotation marks, single quotation marks, etc.

When it comes to single quotation marks ('...'), you can forget it because many people have no clue as to what they are used for. As a result, when we receive manuscript with biblical references requiring double and single quotation marks, we get a lot of very interesting use of them. Also, a lot of writers do not know whether to put the period inside or outside of the quotation marks at the end of their quotes.

Many of writers also have the same problem with parenthesis and brackets; they do not know what to do when they have a scripture reference in parenthesis at the end of the sentence so they put the period after the sentence. By so doing, they leave the information in the parenthesis dangling and unattached to the sentence. This is one of my worst pet peeves and I see it in most manuscripts. As a result, I advise the new writer to read books on grammar and punctuations and to make sure that they pay attention to the correct ways of constructing sentences, learn about the rules of punctuations and other elements that make for mature writing.

Why Use Punctuation Marks?

We use punctuation marks because readers expect to be informed when there is a pause, a deep breath, the end of a thought or speech and when there is an outburst of emotions (e.g., exclamation).

Use of Commas, Dashes, Hyphen, Colons, Semicolons and Periods

The various degrees of a pause are signified by commas, dashes, colons periods and semicolons. You use a comma (,) and a dash (-) <u>to denote a short pause</u>. You use a hyphen (–) <u>to denote a longer pause</u>. When you want to denote a finality, you use a period or full stop(.), a colon (:) or a semicolon (;). When you want to show that something important is about to follow your final statement, you use a colon.

Before you begin another idea, you use a period or a semicolon but you always use a period at the end of each paragraph.

Question Marks: ?
You use a question mark after a question in a sentence.

Example:
Are you on your way home?

Exclamation Marks: !
You use exclamation marks to denote strong passion or outburst of emotions. They follow an exclamatory remark in a sentence.

Example:
How dare you speak to me that way!

Quotation Marks
1. Double Quotation Marks: " "
You use quotation marks to show exact words of the speaker or writer, and to set off the titles of short literary works such as poems, essays, short stories, magazine articles, songs, etc.

Example:

According to John, "Fishing is for the birds."
2. Single Quotation Marks: ' '
You use single quotation marks to set off quoted information when you are quoting the information within a double quotation mark.

Example:
Janice said to me in confidence, "Alice is the most beautiful little girl that I have ever seen but John said that 'she is a spoilt little brat' but I immediately rebuked him for it."

The difference between a dash and a hyphen
A dash: -
A dash is shorter

A hyphen: —
A hyphen is longer. They are both used to denote a pause.

Ellipsis: ...
Ellipsis is used to indicate a break in continuity. The rule is to use only three dots to denote ellipsis.

A lot of people do not know how many dots to use to denote ellipsis, so they use as many dots as they like.

Example of good use of ellipsis:
The scriptures say, "Love your enemies, do good to those that hate you...bless those that curse you."

What the ellipsis show is that part of the statement has been omitted intentionally.

Apostrophes: '
They are used to show **possession, plural forms,** and **where a number or a letter has been omitted.**

Examples:
1. It is **John's** book (it shows possession)
2. We have scheduled the **Writers'** Workshop for next month (it shows the plural form).
3. He **won't** return our calls (it shows that a letter has been omitted).
4. In the **'80s,** music was free of obscenities (it shows that a number has been omitted).

Parenthesis: ()
They are used to set off nonessential information in a sentence.

Example:
His book **(which I am not planning to read anytime soon)** is sitting on my night table.

Brackets: [ ]
They are used to enclose editorial comments.

Example:
He pleaded not guilty to the charges **[but everyone knows he committed the crime]** and his lawyer thinks he can win the case.

Chapter 11

Basic Rules about Editing Your Book

Types of Editing

We have what we call **basic editing** that is focused on correcting minor typos. The basic editing type corrections are for those who have good English skills and require minimum changes or editing. If someone is not a good writer but God gives something powerful to the person and we feel that the world needs to know about it, we do not mind helping the person to handle the writing part of the assignment by providing the person with what we call **extensive editing**.

We do not allow a person's lack of good command of the English language hinder the person's manuscript from being published. This is why when a person who has limited command of the English language comes to us at **To His Glory Publishing Company**, we tell the person that our job is to view his or her manuscript as a diamond in the rough and our duty is to sculpture it, to design it and to make it look beautiful so that God can be glorified by the finished product.

This is why many of our authors call us "miracle workers" because they bring to us manuscripts that other publishing houses will not accept and we actually make them into very good quality readable books! We have had people with manuscripts that contained very bad English and they insisted on "no editing" because they "got the words from the Lord" and no human is supposed to change or edit it but I always tell them that God invented the English language and that He has a superb command of the English language.

Therefore, if the English is all messed up, it is definitely not God that messed it up but the vessel that transmitted the message. As a result, there is no manuscript that cannot be edited. We want to make sure that when people are reading an author's "thus saith the Lord," they are not going, "His God cannot speak good English."

Having said all that, I will again reiterate the point that as a new writer, you need to get some books on grammar before you begin writing because your book needs to be well written. By this I mean that the sentences in your book need to be grammatically correct each time. No one wants to read a book that has sloppy writing.

For instance, I am someone that will pick up a reading material and if it has typos, poor sentence structures, subject and verb agreement issues, etc., instead of my focusing on what the person wrote, I usually find myself editing the material rather than reading it. As I am editing the material, I am not even focused on the person's argument or ideology because the incorrect sentences that I encounter get in the way.

I do not believe that I am the only person that does this because I am convinced that there are many people who are just like me out there. Also, as a writer, you do not want to create an editing job or an editing assignment for your reader because they will miss the point that your book is trying to make.

I cannot stress this point enough that editing your book should not be a default project for those who read your book. Therefore, make sure that you get some books on grammar to help you brush up on your writing skills. A lot of people did not like grammar in school but I was not one of them because I actually liked my English classes. My Dad was known as "Mr. Grammar." As a result, to my elementary school teachers, I had no excuse for making mistakes in my English papers.

The Importance of a Well Written Manuscript
It does not matter what profession you decide to

pursue in life, you will always have a need to write. In most cases, what you write down represents you and your skills. Therefore, if you have poor writing skills, people will always think that you are incompetent in your chosen profession. It is hard to get away from writing in today's society so you might as well learn the rules. As I said before, writing is an art and you can learn it. It is never too late for anyone to learn how to write.

A few weeks ago, we had an author that called about a manuscript and he said that there were no paragraphs, no commas, no periods, etc., in his book because it was in "Black English." According to him, the manuscript was just one long block of writing and he said that he did not want anything changed in it. He wanted the book to be published "as is" without any editing! We told him that English language is not subject to his personal choices and desires even when writing "Black English" because the parts of the book that are not in quotes as "Black English" will still have to be grammatically correct.

We told him emphatically that there are rules in English grammar and the rules must be applied even within the context of his "Black English" sentences.

A year earlier, we had an author that wrote a book in "Black English" and we kept the integrity of the "Black English" but made sure that the entire work (including the "Black English") was written in a grammatically correct form. We told the author that he could keep the "Black English" but the aspects that were not "Black English" should be grammatically correct. In editing the book, we maintained the integrity of the writer by putting the "Black English" in quotes and we made sure that the parts of the sentences that were not "Black English" were well constructed sentences.

Every writer has to know the rules of grammar and

abide by them because those who are going to read the book expect to see well constructed sentences.

How to Save Money on Extensive Editing

I say again that when it comes to editing, manuscripts fall into two categories—the basic editing and the extensive editing. Extensive editing means that the manuscript will require a major editing job to get it ready for publishing. It is the most expensive type of editing because it requires the most work.

I will say here that authors are not the best editors of their own manuscripts. No matter how good a writer you are, you are still bound to make some mistakes in your manuscript because as you look at your manuscript over and over again, you stop being able to see your own errors. Therefore, you need to have someone other than you edit your manuscript once you are done with it.

In order to get around the cost of extensive editing, we recommend that when you are done with your manuscript, you should have someone that has a good command of the English language proof read or edit your manuscript. Therefore, do not submit your manuscript to a publisher without having two or more people edit the manuscript first. It will save you money on extensive editing.

Just because your manuscript was edited by a person with a good command of the English language does not mean that there might still not be more editing that needs to be done in it because only God is infallible. We had an author who paid a professional editor about nine hundred dollars to edit her manuscript and she was surprised when we showed her some typos and other things that still needed to be fixed in the manuscript. She was still able to save some money on editing because her manuscript only required the most basic type of editing. Therefore, be prepared to have your book edited by professionals.

What to Edit For

Editing requires that you read and re-read the manuscript carefully so that you can check for:

- ☐ Clarity
- ☐ Relevance
- ☐ Errors in subject verb agreement
- ☐ Errors in spellings
- ☐ Errors in punctuations
- ☐ Required changes in the manuscript
- ☐ Word omissions
- ☐ Incorrect transitional sentence, phrases and words
- ☐ Incorrect verb forms
- ☐ Inaccurate noun and pronoun usage
- ☐ Weak sentences, etc.

Be willing to eliminate sentences that do not add to what you are trying to communicate or that detract from the point you are making.

Words of Wisdom about Editing

1. Accept the fact that your manuscript might have bad sentences that need correction.

2. Accept that you are fallible and that God does not speak bad English when your book is about what He said to you.

3. Accept the rules of Grammar and do not make your own rules.

4. Avoid weak sentences by using first person grammar because they are most powerful.

5. Avoid wordy sentences.

Examples:
For the known reason that *(bad)*. Instead, use **because** *(good)*.
At this given moment *(bad)*. Instead, use **now** *(good)*.

6. Avoid sentences that are too long.

7. Avoid choppy sentences.

8. Avoid ambiguous writing by making sure that your sentences are very clear.

9. Know the rules about prepositions in your sentence structures.

10. Know the rules about the use of clauses in your sentence structures.

11. Know the rules about subject and verb agreement.

12. Know the rules about commas, semi-colon, colon, parenthesis, quotation marks, etc.

13. Do not make your manuscript an impersonal writing by using too many formal sentences or too many third person sentences.

    Examples:
    Once begun, the building will be completed *(bad)*.
    Once we begin, we will complete the building ***(good)***.

14. Make use of transitional sentences or phrases.

    Examples:
    As I stated in chapter 1…
    In retrospect…
    In addition to…

15. Avoid comma splices.

    Example:
    She is a mother, she is a cook, she is a volunteer fire fighter, she also loves to run.

16. Avoid run-on sentences.

    Examples:
    He is up all night he sleeps all day.
    Girls like pink boys like blue.

17. Proof-read your manuscript and have another person proof-read it also.

I say again that as a rule, you still need another person to edit your work because you cannot be the best editor of your own work.

Conclusion

Having gone through this book, my hope is that you will now be able to produce a very well written manuscript that can effectively convey all that you set out to write about. As I have already said, writing is an art and you can learn it if you truly want to. I have told you in this book the secrets that I think you need to know about publishing and the publishing industry and I hope that the sections on the **Basic Rules of Grammar** and the **Use of Punctuation Marks** were of great benefit to you.

What you need to remember is that your book will continue to echo your view points long after you have gone, so do not let anything prevent you from writing about the God-given topics that are in your heart. As I showed you in this book, you can also position your book to be a great source of financial blessing to you and your family.

After publishing your book, marketing your book is the next important step that you need to take in order to make sure that your book is positioned for mass marketing. Self-published books are not positioned for mass marketing through major book distributors. It is one of the reasons that major book buyers and bookstore stay away from them.

Find a reasonably priced publisher for your manuscript and use the services of good editors. **To His Glory Publishing Company** is always willing to help authors with their manuscript. You can contact us at:

To His Glory Publishing Company, Inc.
463 Dogwood Drive, NW
Lilburn, Georgia, 30047
Phone: **(770) 458-7947**
Email: tohisglorypublishing@yahoo.com

Bibliography

Ogenaarekhua, Mary J. *A Teacher's Manual on Visions and Dreams.* Lilburn, GA: To His Glory Publishing Inc., 2004

Ogenaarekhua, Mary J. *How to Discern and Expel Evil Spirits.* Lilburn, GA: To His Glory Publishing Inc., 2005.

Ogenaarekhua, Mary J. *Understanding the Power of Covenants.* Lilburn, GA: To His Glory Publishing Inc., 2008.

Ogenaarekhua, Mary J. *Keys to Successful Mentoring Relationships.* Lilburn, GA: To His Glory Publishing Inc., 2008.

Ogenaarekhua, Mary J. *Keys to Understanding Your Visions and Dreams.* Lilburn, GA: To His Glory Publishing Inc., 2004.

Ogenaarekhua, Mary J. *Unveiling the God-Mother.* Lawrenceville, GA: To His Glory Publishing Inc., 2004.

TO HIS GLORY PUBLISHING COMPANY, INC.

463 Dogwood Dr. Lilburn, GA. 30047, U.S.A (770)458-7947

Order Form for Bookstores in the USA

Order Date: _____
Order Placed By: _____   By Fax: _____
Address: _____
_____
City _____ ST/ZIP _____
Phone #: _____
Email: _____
Purchase Order#: _____

Return Policy: Within 1 year but not before 90 Days.

Price	Quantity	List Price
Shipping Method:		
Media:		
UPS:		
FedEx:		
Other (Please Secify):		
Total Price:	**Total Quantity:**	**List Price**

Ship To Address: **Bill to Address:**

TO HIS GLORY PUBLISHING COMPANY, INC. • 463 Dogwood Dr. Lilburn, GA. 30047, U.S.A (770)458-7947

To His Glory Publishing

Let Us Publish Your Book

To His Glory Publishing Company will publish your book at the least expensive cost. We pay one of the highest royalties in the industry – 40%! We print on demand and place your book on the major online bookstores such a Amazon.com, Barnesandnoble.com, Bookamillion.com, etc.

WWW.TOHISGLORYPUBLISHING.COM
(770) 458-7947

MARY J. MINISTRIES
463 Dogwood Drive, NW
Lilburn, GA 30047
Office 770-458-7947, Fax 770-458-7947

maryjministries@yahoo.com
www.maryjministries.org
Also check
www.tohisglorypublishing
for your publishing needs

Order Form for Books and CDs

Item	Description	Unit Price	Quantity	Total
	Materials by Prophetess Mary J. Ogenaarekhua			
Bk1	Effective Prayers for Various Situations, Vol. I	$16.95		
Bk2	Effective Prayers for Various Situations, Vol. II	$18.95		
Bk3	A Daily Prayer Journal	$10.95		
Bk4	Unveiling the God-mother	$12.95		
Bk5	Keys to Understanding Your Visions and Dreams	$16.95		
Bk6	A Visions and Dreams Journal	$10.95		
Bk7	A Teacher's Manual on Visions and Dreams	$14.95		
Bk8	How to Discern and Expel Evil Spirits	$16.95		
Bk9	A Teachers Manual on Discerning and Expelling Evil Spirits	$14.95		
Bk10	How I Heard From God: The Power of Personal Prophecy	$12.95		
Bk11	Keys to a Successful Mentoring Relationship	$18.95		
Bk12	A Workbook for Successful Mentoring	$14.95		
Bk13	Understanding the Power of Covenant	$19.95		
Bk14	Secrets About Writing & Publishing Your Book	$18.95		
Bk15	The Agenda of the Few	$17.95		
	CD Sets and DVDs			
Cd1	Visions and Dreams – 6 Part Series (Lessons 1-6)	$55.00		
Cd2	How to Discern & Expel Evil Spirits–6 Part Series (Lessons 1-6)	$55.00		
Cd3	Keys to Successful Mentoring Relationship–6 Part Series (Les 1-6)	$55.00		
DVD1	Dealing With the Strongman in Your Life	$18.00		
DVD2	Looking into the Spiritual Realm and Praying Effectively	$18.00		
DVD3	Understanding the Power of Covenants	$18.00		
DVD4	Understanding Your Visions and Dreams	$18.00		
DVD5	Spiritual Discernment	$18.00		

Shipping anywhere in Cont. US: Add $5 for First Item + $2 for Each Additional Item ($20 for Set1 or Set2)

Please make check or money order payable to Mary J. Ministries.

Total of Products Ordered _____
Add 6% Sales Tax _____
Add Shipping & Handling _____
Total with Tax & Shipping _____

For Credit Card Payment *:

Name on Card: _____ Exp Date: _____

Card #:_____ Card Signature: _____

* We accept Visa and MasterCard

Ship Products To:

Name: _____

Address: _____

City: _____ State: _____ Zip:_____

Phone Number _____ Email Address: _____

All Sales Are Final –Contact To His Glory Publishing Co. for Current Prices at 770-458-7947 or tohisglorypublishing@yahoo.com

EFFECTIVE PRAYERS
FOR VARIOUS SITUATIONS

Prophetess
Mary J. Ogenaarekhua
AUTHOR OF UNVEILING THE GOD-MOTHER

Vol. 1

EFFECTIVE PRAYERS
FOR VARIOUS SITUATIONS
Vol. II

Prophetess
Mary J. Ogenaarekhua
AUTHOR OF UNVEILING THE GOD-MOHTER

KEYS TO UNDERSTANDING YOUR VISIONS AND DREAMS

A CLASSROOM APPROACH

MARY J. OGENAAREKHUA
AUTHOR OF UNVEILING THE GOD-MOTHER